FIVE MORE MINUTES

AN UTOPIC VISION OF A SELENOPHILE

SRI CHAITANYA GLOBAL SCHOOL

This work is dedicated to the mortals who've been facing the curses of the society, to the ones who are neglected, to the ones who are tamed, the ones who's lips are stitched and hands are tied. Basically, it is for each and everyone who is abiding in this planet while facing the social issues outside and even inside their households.

Contents

Foreword *vii*

Acknowledgements *ix*

1. Biog 1- Pravat Kumar Sahoo 1

VERSE 1- THE HOUSE EMPRESS

2. Biog 2- Adyasha Dubey 7

WOMEN PERSECUTION

3. Biog 3- Swoyam Pragnya Sahoo 15

ART AND CULTURE OF ODISHA

4. Biog 4- Abhijit Panda 27

DOWRY SYSTEM- A SOCIAL DISEASE

5. Biog 5- Saishree Subhadarshini 35

HOW EMOTIONS ARE MADE?

6. Biog 6- Smaranika Patra 43

VERY WELL MIND- AASRA

7. Biog 7- Saanvi Parija 55

HUMANITY- CASTE, RELIGION AND GENDER, ABOVE THE ALL

8. Biog 8- Biswajeet Mahalik 67

LOVE THE RIGHT CHEMISTRY

9. Biog 9- Jigyansha Mohaptra 75

DON'T LET THEM DISAPPEAR- THE ENDANGERED SPECIES

10. Biog 10- Satya Prakash Sahoo 83

THE SLOW POISONING OF THE ARCTIC- THE POLLUTION

11. Biog 11- Abhignya Arpit Pradhan 91

YOUR BRAIN THE SMARTPHONE AGE- SCIENCE: A BOON OR CURSE

Contents

12. Biog 12- Rohan Pattanaik 99

"ODISHA"- THE LAND OF TEMPLES.

13. Biog13- Hrishita Das 109

HINDU TEMPLE AS A SOCIAL INSTITUTION

14. Biog 14- Rahul Dev Bera 119

PREHISTORIC- THE SHRINE

Sri Chaitanya- The Flame Of Education 127

A Page Of Response And Views, If Any 129

FOREWORD

DR. SASANKA SEKHAR KANUNGO (DIRECTOR CUM PRINCIPAL)

Absolutely it's incredible that the team has defined their talents through ballad, bullets instead. It's a fact that the book is in the pain that the team declared by representing their practical wisdom. We express our blossom of thanks to the entire young chaps for their elegant efforts and energetic Endeavour. We extend our salute to prof. (Dr.) S.S. Kanungo for his outstanding ideas . It's an immense pleasure for the learning opportunities have been printed by the team.

All impossible have been transferred into possible only for education. It is the fond store of activities. A nation can be succeed to stand by its own prosperity because of good education. The vivid design completion of the work couldn't have been accomplished without those chaps. They have kept the countless timings during the hectic schedule shall never be wasted. The

cooperation and coordination signifies the reality among the little minds are much appreciated and duly noted.

In the Sai Chaitanya the nectar spreads and recollected a handful of golden seeds from the smiling lips. In a very moment I myself concepts the supreme feelings with divine soul. Love and live in love is the fundamental ingredients of the sagacity.

ACKNOWLEDGEMENTS

This work would not have been possible without the dedication and support from our lovable director cum Principal Prof. (Dr.) Sasanka Sekhar Kanungo, who has been supportive for the career goals of the students and who worked actively to provide the students with the protected academic time to pursue their goals. And the institution is especially indebted to JPC MISHRA ma'am , and all the members of Notion Press. The institute is grateful to all of those with whom it has had the pleasure to work during this and other academic related works. Each of the members of the publication Committee of the Sri Chaitanya Global School, Tomando, Bhubaneswar have provided extensive personal and professional guidance and taught a great deal about both scientific research and life in general. The institute would especially like to thank all the teachers. They have taught the students more than they could have been given credit for, here. Most importantly, I would like to thank the parents who have provided unending support to publish the book.

I

BIOG 1- PRAVAT KUMAR SAHOO

All impossibles have been transferred into possible only for education. A nation can succeed to stand by it's own prosperity because of good education. Growing with the high and low tides of the ocean, my days of youth were spent, learning the art of the Pearl formation from a drop of rain. With a vision to deliver

quality knowledge to as many souls as possible, this determined soul succeeded in adding the prefix, "Prof." To his name. Alike the dawn that fills your environment with bright rays; Pravat, makes sure to turn every frown into a grin with his efforts. Young chaps being his favorite inhabitants, he sees his own victory in their triumphs. In the gardens of SCGS, from the nectar spreaded, handful of golden seeds collected; he believes to have found the supreme link with the Divine soul. Love, live in love is the fundamental ingredient of the sagacity.

VERSE 1- THE HOUSE EMPRESS

She never sits on a throne

Never wears a crown

Never order's anyone

Never visits alien

But watches

Not entertains

But interprets in the reign

She never dreams the rainbow

Never feels shy

No urg or smile

No compiles

Never visits abroad

Ever her father's house

Yet too long her exploring

Sings, swings and summarising

Loving and caring

Till cradel to grave

All that she adores

That impress

The real house empress.

VERSE 2- NO RAIN, IN THE RAIN

No rain in the rains
No gental patting
No drops even
It's something new
As if summer season,
It's exhausted
Changing the earth
Cool the warmth
Unbearable the race
No grasshopper dancing
No sparrow chirps
No crickets noises
Nothing inthe ways
Losing grips
All seems display
All slip away.
Yeah.....
It's mournful,intolerable
It's elegiac mood
No joys no guys
Caught the hearts with errors

It's forest fire
As if something undone
No rain in the mountain
The rivulets seems empty
No gross in the meadows
Cornfields dried up
No life in the woods
Livings broken
No rain in the ground
No clouds sound
The rainbow left the horizon
It's summer....?
No water or cooler
No rain in the water.

II

BIOG 2- ADYASHA DUBEY

Amidst the ranges of Gandhamardhan,her consolation as soothing as the sanjeevani's medication,her smile as bright as the

leuciferine of the firefly,this 4'll is really adorable.Although she finds herself aimless at time's, her unceasing determination to create a path towards her goal is quite strong.she believes her aim to be the oxygen without which ,no life sustains.For her ,dance opens channels of peace.At the end of an eventful day,dance becomes the medium of relaxation creating a tranquilising effect.The beautiful scene of descending rain drops ammuses her.Music puts a break to a long chain of complex thoughts.Her ambition to become a better person revolves around the inspiring life stories of nation hero's.Ranging from the chirp of the birds to the tune of the guitar,from the resulting of leaf to the jingling of tambourine,music has been her source of Rejuvenation.The inspired and the dedicated Adyasha wants to gleam brighter than the sun and fly like a free bird in the open sky.

WOMEN PERSECUTION

"Relax! Relax! You have to be strong". Have patience the midwife tried to comfort her, the cries of a to be mother was echoing all around. Suddenly, the pitch of the cries changed. A new soul had entered the face of the earth. The mother heart was delighted at the first sight of her daughter. She felt a sense of completeness. "You are finally here, my love", exclaimed Rebti, but the face of her family members depicted dissatisfaction, as the soul also had a womb.

"Sulekha! come fast and clean the utensils and help me to was the clothes off, and afterward bring vegetables from the market", said Rebti. I said "OK" with a sad expression. I went to the market, where I met my friend Ganga. "How are you?", Ganga asked. I replied, "I am fine and what about you?", She replied that she is fine, She was all the time seemed to be doughtful about something which made me curious. I questioned how her parents allowed her to go to school."How school is?"

I have been taught from my childhood that being a girl you are not entitled with any privilages of upperclsass such as co-education. She replied, her parents allowed her to study, to build a good future. "Wow! I am happy for you was said but in unsaid I spoke to myself what kind of pleasure is this". After I took some vegetables and started moving towards my home. I realised in the way that my parent's would never say for my studies which turns a curse for me that I can't study just because I am a girl. Why this discrimination? Doesn't a girl posses any right to acquire knowledge? I decided to convince myself this is my fate and simultaneously my Iris were searching for a route which will be full of own possessions. I reached home and went to talk to my parents. "Ma! Papa! please listen I want to ask you something and I went towards them and I asked that whether I have the rights to study or not. He replied,. you are a girl and generally they don't deal with studies. Without any more discussions I agreed and went away from the room. I thought that why shouldn't I have taken birth in an other family where they would allow the girlsto study but I have no other option now. At the evening time, I heard my parents talking about my marriage with the men of 38 years. Where I am just 16 years. The morning of the day after tomorrow my parents called me to have an important talk. "Sulekha! now you should get marry and a marriage proposal had already reached to your door steps", My father said. I felt hesitated by listening his words. I am thinking of my condition that how my marriage can be done.

It was already 5.00 PM and I was playing on the backward with Ganga. Sulekha! Go and get ready first they will be reaching within half an hour. Sulekha, please be well behaved infront of your new family. So, I got ready for it. They arrived in a white car, with a well dressed manner, they all were behaving very politely with me as if they were cmy real parents.

At the age of 16, I became the bride of a man who was more than twice of my age. The hands which were supposed to make her first cup of tea were now assigned with the responsibility of a whole house.

The moment I saw him, I felt like my whole life is going to be ruined, the look on his face was confusing. He seemed a bit drunked and that smell was so rubbish that I run to my room. And I didn't open my door until they were gone and was hoping that my parents will turn down this relationship.

While looking outside my window, I saw there a car vanishing out of my sight gradually. Then I heard a knock on my door. It was my mother, she seemed pretty happy and that thing really broke my little heart. They did all the rituals that have to be done before the marriage, I was like a tongue- tied dummy, who was being treated as an abstract material.

Everything went roughly. And the day of wedding was right infront of the door and some parts of my emotions were shutting the door tightly.

The day came "In my imagination I had thought of some fairy tales wedding, but the reality was something else. At a same time I was laughing on my imagination, while was crying seeing the reality. That day I saw his face, it was like I am marrying with my uncle. Everything went roughly again. Literally I was not hoping for this. I knew my family background is not well establised so, I had not expected much but it was worse.

My first day as a wife and a daughter-in-law . It went quiet good, Every body behaved and treated me nicely. Even though it did not felt genuine. Gradually with passing of time they showed their real colours. " I can call them chameleons by the way!" My little

hands were rugged and the chemicals of detergent used to was clothes and dishes nearly got scares on it. They began to act abnormally, acting like they don't care about me and behaving rudely.

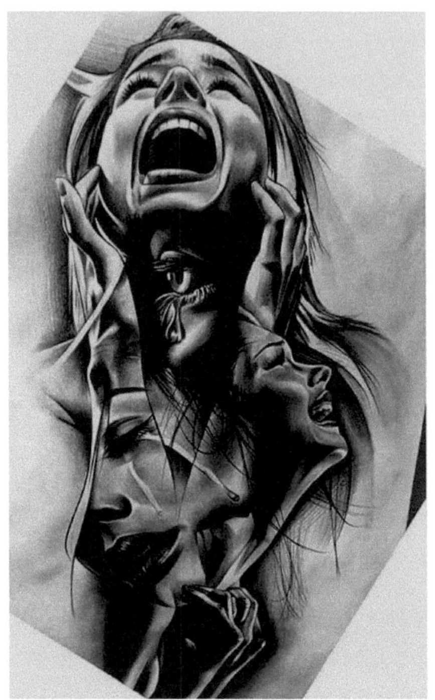

I genuinely had no hope of getting any affection from my husband and sadly I was right. He just treated my like a rubic cube. I have to obey all his words.

He used to beat me and his shoutings now seems to me as normal as day and night.And it was no longer thest. I got to know "I am

pregnent". I was having a mixed reaction,at some point I was happy about it and at some point I was crying deep inside I am going to be a mother at the age of 17 while my old friends were in school at this age.

Suddenly everyone's appearance was changed towards me they act like a bunch of saints but again deep down I knew it was just for some short period of time. I realise that they were all excited for a boy child .Even I was told several times that "I gonna give birth to a very healthy boy ".After hearing this several time I was sured that they will not accept a girl child .At this moment my night mares began and they started to eat me up from inside .That"what if a girl is born?"That "what if " took away my sleep and suddenly I was scared.

And the worst happened my night mares came to reality at 6th month of my pregnancy. I got to know that it is a girl.Again as like the tide changes the change their behaviour and started to treat me as garbage .And even they started to beat me and scolded me very harshly. And treated me for abortion. But I gathered my courage and ran away from the house. People started to judge my decision,said that I am a fool and even raised questions on my character that how can I be a single mother at the age of 17. I with a lion heart hold my emotions and gave all tha possible facilities and affection that i had not received from my parents.

After years; (time skip)

And now I am standing here with all the answers raised by the society about my decision. I am Sulekha a proud mother with a child of 21 and her mother that's me of 38 having the happiest day of my life as being a audience and realising that I gave birth to as IAS officer. And I damned proud to be called her mother.

The story reflects the cheap mindset of some people and pain of women who is being harashed in many ways and still hearing the capability to control all the difficulties.

III

BIOG 3- SWOYAM PRAGNYA SAHOO

Her heart faces the waves just like shores does, with a shaking but tranquilising note. The path of her life was full of hurdles. But the noise of the sea oozing on the shore at silent hours of night

washes all her worries off. The thought of serving the people in need and being addressed as doctor is something which always keeps her motivated. This girl with an appearance as the shade of the lightest cloud is more like a Dorami, who never fails to stand by someone at times of miseries. Being someone as sweet as the fragrant night blooming flowers, she shows a behaviour as the jaggery mashed. "Swoyam", herself more than enough. Painting becomes a way of distraction when she's overwhelmed with storms of emotions. An affiable 5 ft of SSCGS wants to reach the untouched height of success.

ART AND CULTURE OF ODISHA

"Tara ! Tara ! get ready the guests will be here soon", I heard a voice.

My eyes still shut, I was wondering who was being called.

Suddenly I felt someone shaking me and trying to wake me up.

With fluttering eyes and a blurry vision, I saw a well built masculine figure, seeming like a man's.

No sooner than I realised that he was my husband.

"Emma, freshen up, mother in calling you", he said gently.

"Umm... calling ? me ?", I said in a slow voice while rubbing my eyes.

"But... who is Tara then ? " I added.

"That's you !" He replied with a smile.

"Me ?" I questioned, still confused what was going around.

"Oh ! Oh ! you that's me. I'm so... I'm so sorry", I stammered.

"It's Ok dear", saying this he held my face with both of his hands and came a little closer, I felt as if my face was burning hot. Knowing his intentions well, I pushed him a little away and ran into the washroom.

After a while, I came out wearing a bathrobe and with all my hair wet.

"Come sit, let me help you with your hair", saying this he made me sit on the couch and started wiping my hair dry.

"Hubby ! Do I need to wear that long cloth ?" I enquired.

"Are you talking about saree ?" He said.

"Yes sarry" I repeated in my American accent.

"Not sarry baby, it's saree", he gigged while correcting me.

"But I don't know how to wear it !" I exclaimed.

Pinching both of my check with his hands he said, "When will you learn to use meee.... ?", "Don't worry I'll help you wear it" he added.

"Are you sure you can make me hear it ?", I said doubtfully.

"Sure ! why not ? You can always rely on me baby", he said with a smirk.

I agreed as I had no other option.

Then he went near the wardrobe and opened it.

"Oh god !" I exclaimed in amazement.

The wardrobe was filled with different varieties of beautiful sarrys !... Oh ! sorry, 'sarees'.

"Choose one of these and I'll help you wear it", said my husband.

"Oh ! my goodness are these all called as sarees !", I said.

"Yes, but of different varieties !", he replied.

"Varieties ?" I said surprised.

"Hmm..., such as those two are Bamkei Paata, these three are Sambalpuri Paata and that orange one is Kotpat Paata & this yellow one has Bania Bandha work...", he went on.

I will like, Oh god, so many varieties !

But the one I choose was the yellow was the Bania Bandha work saree.

"Fine then, let's go with that yellow one", I said pointing out the saree.

"Good choice ! as always", he said smiling.

"Like ?", I said making my eyes smaller.

"Umm... like... like me !" he said and started laughing.

I laughed along with him.

Then he started to drape the saree around me.

Finally... he said, "Done".

I went to look into the mirror, I felt as if it was someone else standing in front of me.

"How do I look ? ", I asked.

"It suits you well, sweetie...", he replied with a smile.

"But...", he hesitated.

"But what ? Do I look strange ? Is something wrong ?" I said nervously.

"No... But I feel on if something was missing", he murmured.

"Missing ? What ?", I asked.

"Umm... wait", saying this he opened the drawer of the dressing table and took out a few things. Then he asked me to come a little closer and then pressed something on my forehead and said that it was called as Bindi and then applied sindoor and said, "These are the identity of an Odia bahu, you should never forget to wear them".

"Ohk", I agreed.

Then he asked me to sit on the couch and then he bent down and made me wear a silver chain on my ankles, called as 'Paunji' Odia and a toe ring.

After a while, he took me near the mirror and said, "look, don't you feel as if you are the most beautiful woman in the entire world".

He was somewhat correct. I looked quite beautiful with sindoor and mangalsutra as if they enhanced my beauty even more.

The tradition of Odisha is quite special.

"Let go down, everyone must be waiting for us, sorry especially for you", he said with a naughty smile.

It was my 'muh dikhai' program, a tradition of Odia people that when a new bride arrives, the relatives and neighbors will come and see her face by lifting up the veil and then give her gift and blessings for her happy married life.

The toe ring was pricking my fingers as I walked.

Everyone's eyes turned towards me as I entered the living hall, where all the guests and family members were already present.

All my family members were startled when they saw me in saree.

"You look quite beautiful Tara", said my mother in law.

"Thank you Maa", I replied with a smile.

A place was decorated nicely, where I had to sit and one by one all the elders would see my face and give me money or gifts as their blessings.

Many guests came, blessed me and complimented my look as 'Odia bahu'.

I felt as if it was the best decision to live in Odisha after marriage.

"Bhauja..." I heard a sweet voice, which means 'Sister-in-Law' in English.

It was my only Sister-in-Law, Ayisha.

She came and sat near me and said, "You must be bored of these things right ?",

"Do you want me to bring some snacks for you ?", She added.

"No, No dear, I don't feel like eating now. And moreover I am enjoying these things", I replied with a smile.

"Bhauja... my friends want to click some pics with you. shall I call them ?" she asked politely.

"Pragnya, Reema, Kriti, Arushi, Madhabi..." she called them in a loud voice.

They all came, talked sweetly and clicked many pictures.

"How did you fall in love with Aarav Bhai ?" questioned Reema.

Looking at her curious eyes I said, "Umm... fine then listen. I and your Aarav Bhai were University classmates. We studied in the same university in Florida. We eventually fell in love and decided to get married...". I went on.

Aarav, my husband is someone with high virtue and is very well mannered. The he respect the women, elders & even his love and care for the children quite impressed me.

"Let's start with the Ring search", Mamata aunty's voice interrupted my thoughts.

"Ring search ?" Whose ring is lost, I questioned.

Suddenly everyone burst out in laughter.

"What is it ? did I say something wrong ?", I said confusingly.

"No Beta, 'Ring search' is not what you think, it's a ritual of Odisha that every newly married couples perform". said Aarav's grandmaa, Oh ! now she is my grandmaa too !

In a while they made me and Aarav sit face to face and kept a large vessel filled with milk and rose petals floating on its surface, then Ayisha came and showed us a golden ring and then dropped it into the vessel. Then she asked us to search for ring with our right hand.

Eventually I got the ring first.

After all the rituals got over and all the guest departed.

I went upstairs to my room, got fresh and slept as I was quite tired.

Thus the next day we planned to visit the Lord Jagannath temple of Puri.

I and Ayisha sat at the back seats of Inova while Mother-in-Law and grandmaa sat in the middle seats. Aarav drove the car and Father-in-Law sat on the front seat. We were out for Puri.

"Ayisha can you say, that... why do Mother-in-Law, Father-in-Law and grandmaa call me in another name ? Ta...Tara right", I asked curiously.

Ha.. Ha she laughed and then said, It is a custom of Odia family that when a new bride arrive, the family accepts her as a daughter of the family. So, they give a new pet name to her out of

love and affection.

Finally we arrived at Puri.

The famous Rath yatra here is known as chariot festival at my place.

Lost in deep thoughts, I didn't even realise, when we reached the Sri mandir, Lord Jagannath temple.

I stepped on the first stair out of the twenty two stair there. I felt as if something was different. I felt a sense of devotion, a sense of calmness even if it was crowded there.

As soon as we entered there, The Chanting of Mantras, the noise of holy bell, the sound of holy conch, the smell of incense sticks

and the glaze of holy Diya filled the atmosphere with divinity.

Odisha is a place which holds numerous number of temples. Here, the sun rises on the land of temples.

Finally we returned home after the darshan. It was a divine experience.

A few days went by, but Odisha and odisha's people never failed to amaze me. The delicious sweets and delicacies filled my heart with the nectar of love. I became a gourmand gradually as Odisha's food posed me all over.

The aroma of delicious pitha-panna, special type of dishes in Odisha, fills the atmosphere during special occasions or festivals.

This place my God ! Is piece from heaven.

One fine evening, I was standing in the balcony and enjoying my coffee while listening to the bird's chirp.

I felt someone hug me from behind, It was Aarav.

"Are you bored here ?" he asked.

"Not at all, I really like this place a lot", I replied with a smile.

"Then do you want to know a little more about this place ?" he asked.

"My pleasure", I said excitedly.

"Fine then come with me let me, let me introduce different kinds of art works of Odisha", saying this he held my hands and took me round his house and said, that maximum decorative items in the house were hand made ! It was quite a shock. I was getting

more and more curious.

"The large wall hanging of Lord Jagannath in the centre there is called as 'Pipli applique' ", He said pointing it out.

"The vase on the teapoy is called as 'Kaincha craft', and that bird's nest decorated there is 'Coir craft' ", he went on.

" Those are horn work right ?", I pointed.

"Yes, you are correct", he replied with a smile.

I was so amazed that Odisha's people are not only filled with culture but also are quite talented.

"Oh ! Oh my God ! It's going to hit 6.00, the evening", I screamed.

I need to give incense sticks and lamp the holy diya in front of the sacred Tulsi plant and l loved to do so.

I hurried down stairs and completed the evening puja.

The Art and Culture of Odisha indeed astound me. I never felt regretted about my acculturation as the Aura that Odisha and the people of Odisha hold is unparalled. In short, Odisha has proved to be an heavenly escape for me.

IV

BIOG 4- ABHIJIT PANDA

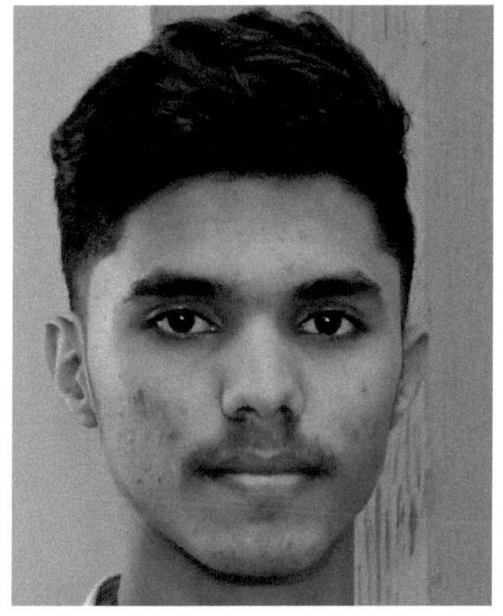

Sky looks great; bright and blue, but it is better when it is dark; full of stars.

Riding the bike, chumming around, clamouring all the way, making the circle aware, the quirky "Abhijit" has arrived.

Simple games don't fond him much but the halucinating world

does. Entering the world of games, being the protagonist, waking down the street with a rifle in hand and a sword at the back, incarnating the soul of a devil, destroying the universe.
And all of a sudden, found himself surrounded by a bunch of frosh at SCGS, it was horrible realising that his world of halucination was broken.
Now in the world of commener's he wants to become the one whom everyone admires, for this he does hardship, day and night.

DOWRY SYSTEM- A SOCIAL DISEASE

Please bring the garland of flowers and ask mamaji,if the sweets's are ready. I picked up the bunch of garland and ran forward the wedding hall. It was beautifully decorated and filled with the aroma of different flower's. An aroma of delicacies filled the atmosphere.Everyone was in the mood of hurry along with an inner excitement except for one ,my sister,Roohi.

Be ready the makeup artist is arriving soon.
" Just 5 minute" Roohi said
My heart is full of bliss.I won't need to share my room anymore . No one would pull away the curtain of the window.The wardrobe would be mine completely. My blakent's won't be pulled off.... Blanket's! who would fold my blanket's for me ? Who would finish of my glass of milk when I'll refuse to ? And who will run

after me with a broom in her hand ? Who's hair would I pull? Whom shall I irritate? I sat back down on a stair . My eye's started misting over . I had never felt my heart so heavy ever before . I some how tried to hold my emotions within myself and put a smile on my face , because at the end of the day my sister is going to start a new journey of her life where for the first time I'll be not with her . So for making her last day special, I'll try my level best to make it memorable with esstasy, jolly and cheerful mood all were enjoying,but there is a person who wore a mask of fake happiness but deep down I knew that my father was deeply unhappy from his inner consciousness. So, I became much more curious to know about his problem . suddenly a call rang bhrum....bhrum...and my father picked up the phone and entered in a room . As I was curious about his hurdle, I went to hear the conversation.I went near the room window where I can listen his voice clearly. "Mam, it is very urgent for me and I will be visiting you tomorrows evening ". My father requested to the mam.

His eyes were dwelling with fear.

I ran into the room where he was talking and suddenly smiled when I appeared.

"What happened? Why are you sad ? With whom you are talking with ? Are you fine Pa " I asked seriously "Nothing much better " he replied." Don't be afraid till I am with you " he added.

" Please don't hide from me " I asked with the confused face.

" Not as a elder son but as a upcoming chairholder you should know the truth " my father exclaimed with sorrow - He continued " The marriage of your sister is not a simple as it look from outside . The in-laws of your sister are demanding a huge dowry i.e jwellery,money,land properties etc. "And suddenly became silent".

I understood the reason of his silence and made my mouth shut and stopped questioning any more .

I was to astonished by looking how a father can sacrifice all his savings which he had saved for his future wellbeing.
While philandering from the room , outside I saw my sister we heard the each word of the conversation.
I saw her eyes filled with tears .
Looking that I tried to convince her and was to say something but she ignored me and run away from there. After her I also started running to see what she was going to do ."I'm gem of my parents, that they have given to you . Don't you think that's enough ? But you are still demanding dowry just for a little luxury. If you are little educated then you must be well informed about dowry system being banned. Just for a few greeedy people like you ,the society is taking girl as a burden .who do you think a girl is ? A girl is someone who can lift up the burden of the entire family all alone ." Roohi shouted. Then I went closer to her end grabbed her hand from behind."What are you doing Roohi? Why are creating a scene here ? Have you gone crazy ! Stop it . " I wishperd." Please don't mind her word's,may be there in some misunderstanding" I explained to the crowed .
"Miss understanding ! What is there to misunderstand here bhai" ? She shouted ." What's the need ? If the financial crisis are so high . Why do we need to give dowry in this condition . I won't get married. It's not compulsory to have a husband .I can live independently " , she said " she is correct " .came a voice out of the crowd , a tall man formally dressed took a stand for Roohi , It was non other than her fiance, Arjun .Then everthing was sattled . "There would be no discussion about dowry any further", he declared , " No ! It is not possible , there will be no marriage if there is no dowry ." Said Arjun's Mother angrily. Then suddenly Arjun walked towards Roohi and hold her hand ." Maa, why are you being so greedy ? Do we lack money ? Don't I have a job ? Then why are you still not satisfied? We are well educated enough not to commit a crime and taking dowry is consider a big

crime ." Arjun explained patiently . Her head bent down in shame and her mother became speechless at that moment as she realised how mean and greedy she was . Fine let's proceed with the marriage .

The beats of drum ,the rhythem of clarenet filled the atmosphere with joy and harmony.

" BARAAT, BARAAT" sounded everywhere in the house .

With the chant's of mantras the ceremony started ,flowers falling on the wedding couple made the environment special.

After all the rituals got over it was time for her Bidaiii. All the family member came to drop her near the car .While entering to the car her eyes were searching for her brother everywhere. When finally she enters into the ear she saw me running towards her . I went near the car and gave her a packet which was nicely wrapped "open it when you reach home". I said with a smile on my face . After all the ceremonies were over, we all returned back to our home. Everyone was having a pack of feelings piled up. Along with a sense of happiness and satisfaction they were also full of grief as the daughter of the house was now the daughter-in-law of another clan. Women with half washed off makeups, smudged and swollen eyes, sat lifeless on the couch. It was a really funny sight. In fear of bursting into a loud laughter, I ran upto our...... Oh! Sorry. My room. I shut the door behind me, climbed up on the bed and laid there out of tiredness. A few minutes later, "Roohi, get me a glass of water. Roohiiiii, I'm tired. Quick. Please." Saying this I sat back up. The mess of clothes, make up stuffs and mainly the jewellery was lying everywhere and that's when I realised, Roohi was gone. The room seemed dead. There was no reply to my orders anymore. My pet, my companion, my enemy, my saviour, My Roohi was not with me anymore. A drop of tear fell on my hand, I wiped my eyes off and went back to the hall

ꟾ

V

BIOG 5- SAISHREE SUBHADARSHINI

Surfing through the high tides and splashing the water amongst her peers , she grew up coming from a Port Town , the coastal breeze having not let her get blonde , but the marine air is

unmatched for her . The tunes of guitar never let her feet , stay at one place . She holds a grin wider than two banks of Ganges , with two incisors popping out like of a rabbit's . "SAISHREE", a Virgo ,holds high aspirations and optimism . Her tongue not less than that of scissors , does partiality to non . With a marvellous sense of fashion , she tends to reach great heights in the future . A super accessible fellow , having endless love for great food . A settled bag-pack would be her favourite things , for she loves visting new places . The giggles of an infant is her favourite sound . Her life at SCGS , took the most dynamic turn , adding the required pinch atrociousness , two tea spoons of boldness and complete bowl of sense of farce .

HOW EMOTIONS ARE MADE?

The loud noise was pricking through my head . Yet again I was forcibly drag into the night club . Raghav slides a peg towards me . "I don't want any" I said . "It will be the first and last , I promised " committed Raghav . I glared at him. "come on Veer ! Since when have you turned so boring ? " he said "Fine, pass it on " ."That's like Veer Malhotra ! he exclaimed pushing the glass. I gulped down in a one go bitterness rain down my oesphagous reintroduction me he the addictive burning sensation. it is consider addictive for a reason . "One more ! quick " The second one blunted my sensory neurons a bit . The third , the fourth and the rest unknown . As a result of which my cerebellum started dis-functioning .

I walked out of the club , trembling some how reached my car, I pushed the accelator pulled the gear and left switched on the woofer and getting drowned in the sea of my memories swaying to the beats of faded ,I felt here fingers tracing mine while my hand shifted the gear, " sara please stop, you are distracting me " . I said looking decided me and to me surprise there was no one

present over there . Without a second thought , I applied all my force my leg head and teared apart through the layers of air ahead me. Out of nowhere a pair of head lights flashed into my eyes. I lost control and crashed into something . Fortunately I was slightly hurt at my head but in perfect condition to drive further, with that I went away.

I woke up to the lyrics of "Night changes". My phone was ringing, it was some unknown cell number. The voice enquired ,"Veer" ."Yes", I replied. "your mother is admitted at the capital hospital, reach there as soon as possible." My heart seemed to skip a beat . Without wasting given a second I rushed to the hospital. The receptionist informed, " a person of around fifty, arrived in hurry, layed down the lady on the strecaher and left ". My world seemed to stop. How could a person be so ruthless and harsh on his on wife? Without thinking much, I filled up all the formalities and' paid the fees using my father's debit card which I had stolen a few days back. As soon as the red light glowed, in a furious aura, I left the hospital. There was sign that read, "no parking", right beside where my car was pulled up. Without even a single hint of formality, I pushed open the front sdoor of my father office and tottered down the main hall into the corridor who's last door read, "Anirudh Malhotra, director cum chief " . I pushed his door with all my force and reached for his collar, "how dare you ? who the hell do you think you are to beat mom to such an extent that she is hospitalized ? " I shouted. To my utter disbelief, he spoke words coated with venom, "I am her husband, I own her. I can do whatever I wish to. No one has been provided with the rights to stop me."

With utmost disgust and unbearable anger, I punched him on his face.It was so hard that his nose started bleeding. He called for his bodyguard who held me by my arms. I was fluttering like an encaged bird." Leave me. How dare you? I will kill you today." I was repeating."Shut up and leave you ungrateful brat. You are being able to walk around the streets just for my money.Get lost". And I was thorned onto the street. My fingers clenched into fist which could dig holes wherever they'd fall. I stood up within a fraction of seconds my fist broke down the glass door at the entrance into pieces, leaving me with blood coated knuckles.

The scene at the hospital seemed to be a bit stable.Mom was shifted to the ward. As I went into it,the doctor depicting a divine figure stood there. "How's she now?" I enquired. "All good just bits of unhealed wounds". The words sounded like taunts. Paying least attention to them, I went on thanking the doctor. She,with a smooth smile said,"It's my work,dear. When I treat someone good,I believe God will help me in some or the other way. In a similar event, my daughter was hit by a car last night. I heard some drunkward was driving it. "The flashlight from the past night flashed across my brain. With all the courage I had, I enquired. "Ma'am,where?". "Near the People's lounge, 5 lanes down from shine forum." My heart stopped. The only things I had in my mind from yesterday's incident were the white letters in bold reading, "PEOPLE'S".

Hearing all the words from the doctor, I realized that I became pulled by hate nated of myself. I felt so much bad about what has done by me. I left from the slight of the doctor there was nothing I can say, more these was like nothing I can do.

Later when I get down I saw the girl that the doctor has mentioned as her daughter. Without thinking much, I got to her and told her everything what I have done and apologized her. I thought she would be angry on me and I also want her to show me no mercy but the actual opposite happened, she doesn't have any much of expression of my talks, she just says"ok,ok! Don't think about it much. I'm all good" that unaccepted reaction from her made me stood their for a while I just don't know what to do now?. After a while I again said, "sorry" and went away. From there,I just want to help her if I can....

"Is it fun being alone?" I just don't know what is happening now in my life. The person who promised to live with me till his last breath.

Now it feels like he doesnot have any time to even talk to me. Even after that I convinced myself by letting myself a peace of mind by thinking that "He may be busy and when he will be free from his works, he will come to me again" I think those convicing words are only go for me .

I saw him with an another girl in the night club. He was drinking with her, kissing her and later take her to the side rooms . I can't found any convineance words in my mind it isn't working anymore. I drank a lot, lost my mind and there was no one else to go . I got a message from my mom, to come home early but heart has got homeless. I feel like there is no one else to go.

With a sudden, the thought of feeling this world came to my mind, I started walking one step at a time even if I die no will get a hurt feeling as no one cares about me even.In blink of light a car stuck me , my legs got injured the thought of learning the world can't be completed as mom's message came again.
The person who accidented me, came near me apologizeme so much, but I don't I'm in a cafe the feeling from my boyfriend are coming to me. I want to be mine I just him right now. I tried calling him several times and at last he picked up, I cried out.
I must have misunderstood him for someone else and asked him about the night club he said "what have you seen is all real and I don't want you anymore in my life , just get lost ".I still just don't know "Is it fun being along ? ".
After that reply from the give, It feel like ' there is no one I can help , no one I can feel assure I'm here. I can't even protect my mother from her dumbass husband " " Is it how life is going to be ".My mother discharge from the hospital and now all better. I want to help anyone and became a better person.
In the cafe , a voice came to my ears that I have heard somewhere. It is a girl's voice , she is crying . I think she had a breakup with her boyfriend. It is a personal matter and I should not interfere in that but I want to help her somehow. I can't hold back anymore " is it how life is going to be ", No I will help her, what will happen , I can leave it for the rest. I stood up from my chair turn back of me . It was the girl I accidented days later.

VI

BIOG 6- SMARANIKA PATRA

Raised in a glorious town set amidst the tall green hill and a peaceful environment in the nature's embrace , filled with its unique tourist sites have let me experience a great youth . The diverse aspect of the contemporary world , be it the spiritual , social and traditional , have always been astounding althrough my

growing years . The eternal blue and the mizzle act like calmatives . Simple yet mind -boggling sentiments usually break a mirror of sensitivity where i have always tried to illustrate my impeccable image . One common statement from my friends at SCGS ,"SMARANIKA is super-companionable but her impassive face can be quite scary ," makes me giggle awkwardly . Lounging on the bed seems like a preferable choice than hanging out , but the idea of visiting new spots flatters me .

Music, the compilation of array of emotions with rhythms of different instruments creates a personal space for the acceptance of life's concept .During the despondency of life , a certain band named 'BANGTAN' helped me to manuever , love and explore myself with the profound messages in their music .

Tasting multiple cuisines never fails to ignite the desire to discover and create its new variants . But a bowl of Maggi comes above all . Sprinkling life to my thoughts through sketching has been my run to . A keenness to serve the mankind has blossomed over the years .For me , becoming an aspiring physician envisions greater opportunities for the purpose.

Above all , i lead a simple life with the objective to be a good human being .

VERY WELL MIND- AASRA

"Why is it always me ? " I questioned myself in the middle of the night as I stared wide at the screen that wrote 'FAILED'. The letters were more prominent than my pessimism could have estimated . The persistent determination since years was finally shattered into nihility . My hands reached out for the knots of my hair, tugging them harshly . I could not think straight .

A tear escaped my eye. Instantly, I found myself sobbing, complementing the heavy rain outside the window . Yet , the velocity of the descending rain drops couldn't have exceeded the velocity of my sentiments running down my face .

Amidst all the evil thoughts, a scene from the previous year popped up in my mind .

"Hey , I think I like girls " I said nervously as i stood in front of my best friend .

"Uhh, what ?"She interjected with a certain unreadable expression painted on her face .

"Yes , I discovered that I am fond of girls ." I smiled trying to be confident .

"Anika , are you joking ? Did Vani give you another foolish dare ? " She giggled.

"No, Ragini I am serious."

Her smile dropped .

"That's not true."

"It is."

"Go to a doctor . May be a psychiatrist too , you seem to have lost your mind. And i think we cannot be friends anymore ." She said and walked away .

Tears of disbelief ran down my face as my lonely, desperate figure stood by the dark alley.

Ragini was the one who had helped me when I was bullied by a group of rude kids at my school . They made fun of me due to my severe entemophobia. I believed she would support me through this too. But , the daggers of her words dug holes inside me; holes that could not be filled afterwards.

I lost my best friend that day , and we have never contacted again .

My heart clenched at the memory .

In matter of seconds, another memory flashed in front of me .

"I am not raising this girl further . Do whatever you want to do. "

" How can you say this for your own daughter ?"

"First of all , I never wanted a daughter."

"Is that really a Heart which is beating beneath your ribs or is that a mere stone?"

"I dont want to see your faces ."

"What?"

"You heard me . "

"Alright then ."

We left my father when I was in the fifth grade . And thereafter, my mother had raised me single - handedly .This entrance exam was all that I had goaled for since years so that i could have been finally be able to support her atleast somewhat.

Her expectant face flickered in my mind . But my disappointment overpowered .

"Am I a failure after all ?" I asked myself .

Whirls of thoughts circled around my head.

Incidents and statements appeared one after another , hitting me like asteroids as I sat staring into the oblivion.

"You are not even close to good ."

"You will fail ."

"You look terrible ."

"You are not a bisexual but rather a psycho. "

"Please pass in the entrance ."

"Boo , you are a looser ."

"Oww , are you afraid of a bug? That's pathetic ."

Voices rang through my ears , sreaming in the loudest pithes and amplitudes .My head stinged as if it was being pierced with numerous knives .

"This needs to end ."And with that , I pulled out my chair , grabbing the scarf lying on my bed. With trembling hands , I looped it and placed it around my neck , tying its other end to the ceiling fan. Sliding the chair away from beneath my feet , I proceeded to strangle myself . The knot around my throat tightened, the cloth straightening immediately.

Everything seem so normal for a few seconds until l could not inhale any more. My fists tightened and toes curled at the breathless sensation in my chest. At some point, my limbs started going numb as my body was chilling slowly, my eyes fluttered close, my vision going out.

Suddenly, a lightning struck, with the thunder being loud enough to pull me back into the reality.

I gasped for air, huffing through my throat which burned. A shiver of terror ran down my spine. I was unable to contemplate the situation.

I saw the same scarf on my bed. I picked it up and glanced at the ceiling fan that was over my head. but my guts didn't let me take any step further. I threw it away and screamed in utter disbelief. My tongue tasted the salty pain, as tears streamed down my face endlessly . The feeling of devastation suffocated me . I squeezed up at a corner, clasping around my shaking body. The night outside was dark but the darker black hole of my mind attracted anxiety and panic stronger than the gravity. Amidst the situation I passed out to the exhaustment of the overwhelming emotions.

The next morning, I saw a face with swollen eyes and smudged Kajal, white lines running down the cheeks. I felt lifeless, yet I got ready for the college.

"Anika" I heard a familiar yet unknown voice. Regardless I ignored it like any other day continuing on my path. "Anika" I heard again but I paid no heed. The voice calling me out for the third time was quite strange. "What is it?" I turned around and looked at the owner of the voice with a rather grim face. His expressions didn't change; the wide grin I had seen often but never responded to. "You look pretty" the guy said. I knew I didn't, not at least with the swollen eyes and a pale face. I continued walking. But he kept following, with his stubborn voice pestering me. Frustrated, I howled at him. "What do you want?"

"Nothing... just a smile on your face" I stared at him. He stared back with a flirty smirk. No exchange of words occurred for few moments.

"I attempted suicide". "What". His expression faltered. I remained silent. Not words but pain gushed out in the form of hot streams of unspoken emotions. I could feel his arms engulfing me in his warm embrace. After holding him tight for what felt like an hour , we finally seperated. He did not question me again as if he understood my silence.

He tugged my hand and led me towards his car. I was too spent to question him about his actions.I followed him nonetheless. The trip remained silent, one that was not awkward but comforting.I kept glancing at the sprinting bulidings out of the glass pane. The car pulled over by a park.

"Anika , Let's get down."He said. I hummed a yes.

He took me towards a bench that was set at the corner of the park. Silence flushed around, the smell of the grasses soothed my heavy heart. I fiddled with the hem of my shirt . He was looking

at the sky.

"I don't want to end my life." A possible shift in his activities could be noticed.

He looked into my eyes .

"Do you want to talk about it?" As expected.

"I hallucinated about suiciding. Not actually trying to kill myself but the scenario was too scray. I never expected myself to attempt something like that."

I fumbled with my words . I felt his hand clasping onto mine , drawing circles on it's back to calm me down.

"I need help. I need to overcome those thoughts. I am required to live ahead and killing myself doesn't sound like the best choice. Wh-What do I do?" . The words were all over the place.

"Hey look, don't panic. I am here, we will find a way." He falls quiet, as he thinks for a few moments.

"AASRA!"

"AASRA?"

"Yes! A helpline that helps people in distress. Maybe they can help?"

"So, I'd need to meet them?"
I asked confused
"No. The counselors can help you over phone. Why don't you give it a try?"
His hopeful eyes looked at me.
"I want to try." I said with a faint smile.

He took the phone swiftly and dialed the helpline number. It rang for a few seconds, until someone picked up the call.
"Hello?" A gentle voice answered the phone.
"Good evening. Is this AASRA?"He enquired. "My friend needed some help."
"Yes, please tell them to talk to us."
He handed over the phone to me.
The counseller on the other side asked various simple questions and I replied accordingly
I could consult about my problems frankly. "Don't bottle up your feelings often. Do share with a person you trust.' I fell silent for a second. After Ragini, I hadn't met another soul who held the label of my 'trust'. And I have never wanted to sadden my mother with what I have been facing.

"Miss Anika, are you there?"

"Y-yeah."

"It's alright. Don't push yourself to think about the circumstances. Do you have a hobby?"

"I guess I do. I like to paint. It realxes me at times."

"Perfect! Go for it when you feel out of the place."

I finally hanged up after a long candid talk. It felt really nice to vent out. Talking to the counsellor made it easy to find ways of coping up with the mishaps. Eliminating the suicidal thoughts was like traversing through the hurdles, with the consistent support of the 'college guy'. He had been beside me through all this, like a companion, a mentor, a brother, a run-to and so much more. It was my journey of learning to handle my sentiments, especially the storms and the tornados that did build up due to the chaotic past I had survived through.

Weeks later, I decided to dial up AASRA, for the final time.

"Thank you for helping me out. And I think I have found the person I can trust with all my heart to share my concerns with, My Best Friend; Shikhar." I said as I smiled at the person seated beside me.

VII

BIOG 7- SAANVI PARIJA

Depicting a bouquet of white and black roses, her eyes hold a daydream of a peaceful and nostalgic world. Not less than a soul from the parallel universe. The crow sitting on the Hemlock tree from frost's "Dust of Snow" met her the other day, quarreling over

a few peers asking, "Are they all fools for loving me?" To which she replied with a smirk, "Never, rather they are great for having a compassion which is unmatched". A Bibliophile, for whom her life is like a Basketball court, where having the best teammates is more vital than being the sole champion. Tickling the strings of acoustic provides immense pleasure to her, while humming the notes of melodies by late Lata Mangeshkar Ji is an escape from reality for her. A session of laughter and tears with her mother over two cups of tea is all it takes to uplift her mood. A clear and passionate Bon-Vivant, who at times turns into an epicurean, broiling various cuisines for her Kith and Kin. "Saanvi, you will set an example and you will be followed", said her parents when she was just 5. SCGS adds up as a factor for her to work on her aspiration, in order to convert the words spoken by her parents into reality.

HUMANITY- CASTE, RELIGION AND GENDER, ABOVE THE ALL

I woke up to the 'Takbir'. It was another morning initiated by listeting to the namaz, since I have been posted at the Sophian district of Jammu. The chilling breeze, entering through my window, forces me to sleep over for a few more minutes every dawn, but the faces of my whining patients didn't let me do that ever. Leaving my bed, I went to the window. Living on the top floor of a three-storey, traditionally built, slope-roofed house was not so bad. My favorite part about it was the clear view of The Jamia Masjid from my room. The sight of hundreds of men, repeating the practices exactly in the same manner, was heavenly.

"Beep. Beep", my microwave indicated that the water was warm enough now for my green tea. Dipping the tea bag and taking a sip I looked beneath my window. Rallies were being conducted like any ordinary day. The scene was not so good. I decided to get ready for the day.

As I was dressing up, I remembered I was out of matchboxes. It was a really difficult task to get my 4 inched Hanuman statue into the house. My landlord, being an orthodox Muslim checked even my sling bag in search of any Hindu artifacts. "It was heck one of an experience", I laughed to myself. Being option less, I used my so-called 'emergency lighter' to light up the incense sticks and left for the hospital.

Some fight amongst 2-3 Buddhists and a few Muslims were going on. "Who gave you the right to force your illogical beliefs over the hospital which is supposed to be secular" asked one of the Buddhists. "And who the hell are you to question us on that? We are the majority here, we'll decide everything! Now wait outside until our treatment is over." Answers a man in white kurta-pajamma, neck-long beard and a white cap. "Aastha. Aastha!" Came a familiar voice. Anjum, the only colleague I was close to, here. A similar mindset and a determination to serve the mankind, irrespective of their caste or religion had made us best of friends over a period of just a month.

"Aastha, Dr. Ahmed is looking for you, maybe there's another delivery scheduled." she said. The idea of assisting a woman, in bringing a soul into this world, contents me like nothing else. Without wasting even a second, I ran towards Dr. Ahmed's cabin. "Aastha, I've got handmade sewaiyaan for you; skipping breakfast isn't really good always, please have some" shouted Anjum.

"Afterwards!" my voice faded into the chaos.

"Dr. Ahmed, may I get in?" I asked.
"Dr. Aastha, please. I have asked sister to set up the OT, Mrs. Fatima has been going through labor since 8 hours. We have gotta hurry up." he informed. I tried hard to prevail my formal, workaholic face, keeping in my inner delight. "For sure sir!" I replied and rushed into the OT. I, Dr. Ahmed and Dr. Ferroze were assisted by nurses in pulling up our scrubs and we were all set for the delivery.

The cries of Mrs. Fatima filled the room. It was her fourth issue as mentioned in her medical case sheet.
Around 45 minutes later, laid in my arms the infant with it's tiny fingers clenched into delicate fists, crying at the highest pitch. "Congratulations Mrs. Fatima, another 'Insiya' has arrived" said Dr. Ahmed. By "insiya" they mean a girl or a female.

Shockingly her face dropped into an anonymous emotion. She started panting and panicking, "Don't inform my in-laws about her, please don't, Allah would shower fortune on you."
I was amazed. A mother....... not happy with her kid........ Does it make any sense? Dr. Ahmed was trying his best to console her.

"Throw her in the dustbin, before you return back home." demanded her husband.
"But sir, she is your offspring. How can you do that to such an adorable princess?" I interjected.
"Miss, you are not allowed to speak between us, mian-biwi. I know how to handle my family. Spending my hard earned money, for a girl whom I would marry off for sure is nothing more than a waste." he remarked.

"Sir, how can you promote such misconceptions? Being a citizen of the 21st century and having such a mindset doesn't suit you at all. If I am standing here today, amongst such great doctors, it's just because of my Abbu." Stated Anjum.

"How many times do I need to repeat the same thing over and over? DON'T TEACH ME WHAT I AM SUPPOSED TO DO!" screamed Mr. Ansari.
I was speechless, his words pricked through my soul. How can someone hold such a disgusting mentality regarding his own daughter?

Dr. Ahmed tried to handle the case and it was decided that the girl would be dropped at an ORPHANAGE.
My heart seemed to stop, her tiny fist wrapped around my index finger at the time of birth seemed to me as if she knew her fate and was pleading me to accept her, to not let her birth, be worthless.

"I will keep her." my voice echoed. Everyone was staring at me in disbelief. Anjum stood there with her eyes wide open and her lips expanding sideways into a slight smile.
"Mr. Ansari, it's decided then. Sign the legal papers and you are free." stated Dr. Ahmed. A sense of relief was clearly painted over Anjum's face. I could also see the indebtedness in the eyes of Mrs. Fatima.
Walking past the street with a baby in my arms, out of nowhere was awkward. But deep down a human within me was the happiest and importantly, satisfied.

"Whose kid is this?" asked my landlord.

"Mine", I stated.

"I can't remember witnessing your babybump!" She said.

"I know. I was never pregnant. She's saved. Today onwards she's my daughter." I replied confidently.

"And whom is she going to call her Abbu?" she asked.

My heart was racing. Off course I knew I was destined to face this particular question, but this early?

"I will not let her feel the absence of a father. An Ammi is sufficient, isn't she? I said.

"Sure she is, but not here in my house." she declared.

"Khala, please don't do this, I beg you." I was devasted. I didn't know what I was supposed to do next.

“Mrs. Mehrin, do you consider this a valid reason to throw her out of your house?” a voice came. To my surprise it was Qureshi Uncle, Anjum’s father.

“We know each other since years, Anjum and Aastha are really good friends, she’s such an innocent girl with a pure heart, after knowing her personally only I had asked you to let her stay at your residence as a renter. Please let her stay ma’am. She has saved an insiya of Allah from being left as an orphan. Is she supposed to be punished for that?”

Qureshi uncle’s words made all three of us weep. Anjum and her family were always there for my rescue.

“Thank you uncle.” I sobbed.

“Always there for you, Beta.” He kept his hand on my head.

18 years passed within something which seemed like a jiffy. Kashvi, grew up into a goddess. Having Anjum and her family always by my side, I raised her. Even though she had the blood of an islamic in her veins, she was so full of love and divinity for Hindu sculptures. Initially becoming a bully of the kids from the muslim community, she learnt to fight for her, herself. Unaware of her identity she had been trying to convince her classmates that religions open gates to versatility. Attending Iftar parties and EID at Anjum’s residence, recieving Eidi from Qureshi uncle and Sana aunty whom she called, ‘Nanu’ and ‘Dida’ and having them with us for Diwali, Holi etc had made her accept the fact that sharing of customs and rituals, can be fascinating. Having no boundaries amongst one another is the true way of living.

"Maa?". "Yess?" I replied. "Maa, can I ask you a question?" She asked.
"Off course, sweetie! Go ahead." I replied

"Maa, I don't mean to make you feel insufficient or inadequate, but I just want to know something."
My heart skipped a beat, I had seen this question coming, but I wasn't prepared for it yet. An ocean of questions had been on my mind since the day I saved the little baby girl from being thrown away.
" Maa! Maaaa! MAAAA!" She jerked me with her hand. "Maa if you are not ready, if you have some other work, I may come sometime later." She said.
"Probably, you want to know about your father?" I enquired.
"Yes, maa." She exclaimed.
The curiosity in her eyes, the excitement clear on her face couldn't make me keep myself from telling all the truth.
"Maa, am I adopted?"
"No! Not at all!" I grabbed her by her cheeks.

"You are my pride, my love, my world, my daughter! You were saved! Saved from being left at an orphanage or even in a dustbin!" She was horrified.
"Papa didn't accept me? Or his family members? Or......"
"No." I interrupted.
"You have a father, but I and your father are in no way connected"
Confusion was clear over her face.
"18 years ago, you were delivered at the District Hospital....." My narration, had her in tears. She hugged me so tightly as if a python was wrapped around me. "I love you maa. I love you so much." she sobbed.

"I love you more darling." I never expected her to accept all this so maturely. I always had this fear of losing my baby, after she gets to know the secret. I had thought she would behave differently with me and my biggest worry was about her religion. But the scene was completely different from my imagination. She handled the fact as if it didn't mean anything at

all.
"Maa, were not you ever in love? With a guy?". Now, I had never expected this coming. I didn't know what to say. I never thought, a question, other than that of her birth, would startle me this much.

" I have!", I said, gathering all the courage I had.
"I was in love, with a guy while I was pursuing my degree in MBBS."
"Then what happened maa? Why didn't both of you get married?" she enquired.
"Every love story doesn't end at a good note, sweetie. Our castes were different. He was from the weavers clan and socially they belonged to the SC category and I was a general.

My family denied to accept him and we decided to run away."
"What!" She interrupted.
"Yes, but on the day we planned to flee, I kept waiting at the edge of the street and he never came. A few days later I found out that he was married off to one of his cousins. My relatives threatened their family to do so, if they wanted their son to be alive. I left the city forever along with the tale of our love."
"Dr. Aastha! Dr. Aastha! Hurry up ma'am, he will die." Came a loud voice through our window. We ran towards it and looked beneath our house.
A man was struggling with his life, trying to breath.
"Maa, Run!"
We reached the street as soon as possible. I ran to the man trying to detect, what was happening.
" It's a cardiac arrest!" He seemed to be in his 50s.

"Save my husband, please save my husband, Allah would shower fortune on you." A familiar voice cried. I turned around, to my surprise, Mrs. Fatima was running towards us.

"Doctor had suggested, not to expose him to loud noise, but these sound boxes being used for the Danga are not ceasing even for a moment. He is Ill, it is fatal to him. Please save him, please save him!"
The wife he was asking to not to get into his house, if she didn't throw away the baby, was begging for his life.
I ran into the house to get my stethoscope. As I returned, to my surprise, the person was already sitting and panting. I was shocked, as in that area no physician other than me lived.
As I walked closer to them I found, Mrs. Fatima, thanking Kashvi and crying heavily.
I was blank. I couldn't believe on the fact which my senses were trying to convey to me. I went to Kashvi and asked, "Who did this? Who gave him back his life?".

"I've learnt it from you maa. Never discriminating anyone and treating them selflessly."
My eyes teared up, I went to that man, who was none other than, Mr. Ansari, My Kashvi's biological father.

"Sir, are you all right?" I asked.
"Far better ma'am. I can't thank this girl enough. She is a farishta sent to me by allah" he replied.
"And you were determined to throw this farishta away, exactly 18 years ago."
His face turned pale. For a few moments he was blank, he didn't know how to react. Kashvi was in tears. Mrs. Fatima, couldn't stop herself from kissing Kashvi all over her face.

"Religion, caste, genders are the boundaries created by humans. Neither Allah nor Krishna has got to do anything with it. You humans are turning into demons. Keep aside your ego, your hatred and the world can be a better place full of humanity."
Saying this I took away Kashvi along with me into the house.

VIII

BIOG 8- BISWAJEET MAHALIK

"A smile utilizes comparatively less muscle function than that of a frown." His biology professor had mentioned this fact during a lecture, and since the moment , he considered it a rule . A guy with his constant efforts to steal a huge grin from the faces of people around him, even during their hours of distress. Initiating his days at SCGS as an ignored fellow, his demand grew as his sense of humour started gaining attention.

"Biswajeet, crack a joke please", started sounding as a tagline. This usually marked man is an expert at hiding his emotions. As a pinch of sodium chloride glorifies the delicacy, stepping into the world of anime did the same to his soul. He has a dream of serving the ailing citizen selflessly. His ATPs fortunately come into action at the most necessary moments. He can be considered, a boy with the best combo of taunts and humanity.

LOVE THE RIGHT CHEMISTRY

It was my first angle of sight in which I saw her. She was really admirable. All I knew, during that period, was my infatuation towards her.

Those were the days of my elementary school, when we were in 5th grade, She was a new comer .As it was the midway of the year, she was unable to cope up with the syllabus designed by our school which made our introduction possible. Out of nowhere, she came, "Hey, Excuse me, can you help me with the portion completed till now". I was literally surprised. All I was thinking about was what to reply her with. "Nothing much, just the last portion of water cycle in Science". I was never a first bencher,

during my elementary school. "I have heard that the basics of life cycle has begun already and you are still at water cycle and she gave a wide smile. For me that smile was like a thread of wool, which started knitting the garment of chemistry between us. In the beginning of our middle school, my grades were hampered like the petrol that has been evaporated which made me suffer throughout the year. Who was more over than average student, is now better paid off in her field. She was the only girl that I was roaming around. All I thought throughout the day was about her. At a point it was the phase of realisation of my love for her.

And I also knew that, she feels the affection that I have for her. But at some point of time she tried to maintain a distance from me and by the end of the year she left the school without even giving me a clue due to which my mind was miserably affected. This moment of my middle school changed my perspective of love and affection

By the end of my High School , It rewarded me with a tag of "Topper" with a high percentage of my academics, I started to grow up I was under graduate when I confirmed my aim and it was about the healing art, which a doctor can generally do. I was very fascinated with the art of healing which attracted me towards it. After I completed my graduation I took admission in the Aithen Healing Institute, Mumbai, where I took a course of reflexology. It is a method of treatment which is used to relieve and cure tension and mental illness with the help of stimulating the reflex points present in our body such as feet, hands, palm, head etc. It was a course of 30 months. I continued my studies and completed my post graduation so for the further studies and training I was sent to CMC Vellore, Tamil Nadu where I started treating people and I also joined an endocrinical research centre where I studied about hormones related to love, affection, hatred etc.

So I decided to put the love under my microscope where I saw that it is not only a feel but also an asset which rests upon the foundation of evolution, biology and chemistry.
Michel Mills, a psychology professor at Loyola Marymount University in Los Angeles says that, "Love is our ancestors whispering in our ears".

According to Science, Romantic Love is not eternal. However, our body releases a hormone Phenyl ethylamine (PEA) which is generally increased in our early stage of out adulthood. When you flash at a stranger and whom you found attractive "PEA" gives you that silly smile and the whistle blows at the PEA factory and when that PEA increment doesn't lasts forever it leads to argument it just acts as a side kick to your love.
However, I came to believe that Love exists in two aspects:

-Scientifically.
- How I felt when I love the way the other one makes me feel.

Days passed, I somehow started my own clinic where I had plenty of people to whom I have cured. In my entire life of treatment career I never got a call for any home dial treatment and it was a call from a brother who wants to heal her sister from get mental illness. So, I arrived the location provided by her brother. I reached there and I took the first view of my patient. As soon as I saw her I could not believe on my eyes Lily was laying on the bed where her hand was connected to a device by a wire with a monitor which was displaying the graph of Lily's mental state and the graph was a kind of straight line with a sliding hit of up and down. My mind turned blank at that moment but I somehow controlled myself and started the process of treatment. I pressed the space present in the left hand between 3rd and 4th finger which will activate glutamate and serotonin which will results in the activation of brain functioning with a hope created by serotonin.

After some weeks of treatment she shows steady recovery so one day as usually at the time of my treatment, I suddenly felt her presence by my side, and I saw that the graph finally shows fluctuation. It was like a jump start for my heart which gave me ray of hope towards her recovery. Then she started trying to open her eyes and after sometime she blinked at me and she tries to hold my hand by being in the bed. I was looking at her and tried to console her.
Moreover I felt like she was mine at that point and after over more six weeks Lily was finally recovered.

Gradually, time passed and one day she invited me for a date so I was elated by her bidding and I accepted it during the way in my car a bunch of thoughts related to her were coming to my mind. So I reached and she looked at me and tended me in an

infantilized way.

In my point of view,

Everyone has a contrasting procedure of expressing love, and everyone needs to experience love in distinct ways. If you know how your partner needs to feel your love and care without having her questioned of , that's the hint of a great and long-lasting partnership.

True Love exists in the present world as well, you must possess eyes worthy enough to find it and it depends upon the strength of the bond which is built on the foundation of trust, understanding, connection and sacrifice. Lack of any of these factors can weaken the bond to huge extent. In short, you must have each other's back.

IX

BIOG 9- JIGYANSHA MOHAPTRA

Bright as the foam, forming over the edge of the waves, she lives by the Bay of Bengal. Her heart holds more nectar than her words do. With her teeth perfectly aligned and her height extremely fine, this chocoholic with glasses is the most carefree soul you'll meet. Just as a Jasmine in the fields of Roses, she can be distinguished amongst a crowd for her superbly cute, Indie

accent. Her eyes reach the sky and wishes to remain there for most of her life. Having the yoke of a fixed-wing aircraft in her hands,she wants to compete with the Aves. This soul with the least cunningness wins over the hearts of people, as an expert. Jigyansha, the curious one, with the most number of questions in her mind all the time, but also with the most amount of fear. While coping up with the hostellers at SCGS, she learnt a lot of dealing and grew up mainly, intellectually a lot. She desires to be accessible and stay cheerful all her life.

DON'T LET THEM DISAPPEAR-THE ENDANGERED SPECIES

"Ohh God!" At last the vacations had arrived. In the scorching heat, I was half cooked on the way back to home. And that egoistic boss, my life was full of such nonsense. All I wanted was the vacation and thanks to God it was finally there. It was time to reincarnate myself as who I had been before the "waste of time job."

"But what now?" I had no idea about how to spend the days, and that to all alone. All my friends were busy at that odd moment of the year. "Ahh! It's so irritating... Really irritating...!" I had a great idea to about taking a nap; it relaxed me.

"Ohh Gosh!" I had almost forgotten the last day of the office was still there. Again the same car, same office and that boss. Apart from the vacation plans, I just wanted to survive the last day. At last, it was all over. Finally, I had plenty time to lie down on the bed and to think about how to spend the vacation.

"Wow!" I just wanted to suit up and jump into the mesmerizing blue sea. The fishes looked beautiful. And then I fell off the bed all of a sudden.

"Wait what!" I was dreaming. My heart almost popped out. Ok, so there I got the plan to spend the vacations. "Google, do the work perfectly." I goggled some places and finally decided to go to the Little Cayman Island because it had scuba diving facilities too. "Great. So that's it!"

I booked a ticket and started packing my luggage at night. The excitement of the trip didn't let me sleep that night. The next day, I went through security check ups, and boarded my flight. The airplane landed in the Little Cayman's airport. I got down the flight and completed all the formalities and proceeded towards the resort I was going to haul at. Next morning, I went in search for a scuba diving trainer. At last I found a trainer named Jack. He started giving training to me and instructed the rules to be followed during diving. Jack gave me a pair of wet suit and all the essentials required. The training started on the third day. Being new in the field of diving, it took some time learn it. On my first day of training, I almost drowned.

It took me three days to learn to dive perfectly. Jack advised me not to dive alone but my curiosity to know the mysterious things present in the deep ocean was stronger. One day, when I reached the training site, I couldn't find my trainer. I looked for him everywhere but he was nowhere to be seen. I asked a person who

was selling nuts along the edge of the ocean. He told me "Your trainer will not come today."

Then I asked, "Why?" "Jack told me that he had some work at his home." He replied softly. As I was excited to see the charming and attractive fishes, I decided to go alone for diving. I took a boat and went into the water and I jumped into the water

While I wandered there, I saw many fishes, but one of them caught my attention. It was a white fish lined up with red strips and it was roaming at a distance from others. It was way prettier than other fishes. It was glowing and when I got nearer to it, with a splash, it got away towards deeper part of the ocean.

I continued to follow the fish. At one point, the fish disappeared. I turned around to return on my route but a sudden realization hit me. I had lost my way. I noticed that it was darker than my usual path. In a second thought, I could feel my feet getting stuck and being pulled down. I struggled in its hold but still my efforts proved useless under the strength of the unknown source.

Then my eyes closed with a sudden gasp, my eyes opened and I was floating in the surface of the water. I was amazed, how could that happen? I was more than 500 meters down but the water but suddenly I was above on the surface. At first, I was scared but when I looked, everything seemed normal. So, I started to swim back to the island.

When I reached the ground everything started to look a bit odd. The tree look unusual and as my guess they were very old plants which are now days almost impossible to be found but the island was filled with all extinct plant .

Then to amaze me more I cross my road with a very odd animal .It was having horns like Reindeer but I was sure that it was not reindeer .Then when I got near and near to the trees .I saw a different type of monkey .It was unusual by its looks and I was sure about the thing that there were no such animals present on the island before. After realizing this, I ran towards the sea jumped into it right away.

When I entered the water, without even any second thought in my mind, I gave all my power and skimmed down. My eyes were amused to see a dolphin, which was in search of her food, companied by her daughter and suddenly they noticed me looking at them. Then she rushed towards me. At first, I was frightened but when she came nearer to me, she started to sniff around and looked at me carefully. Then she 'talked'. Yes, you heard me right. She 'talked'!!

She asked me, "How your race got extinct?" It was unusual and astounding and at first, it was scary. But looking at her, she was so beautiful; I had never seen any dolphin in my life. So, I answered, "No, humans are not extinct, they are all alive."

Then with an amazed look, she asked "so how did you enter this world?" I was a bit confused by her words. Then I asked her," How can you talk?" And the answer shocked me.

"In this world, it is normal for us animals to talk but a human in our is very unfamiliar." She answered. This concerned me.

As if she could sense my discomfort and tension, she took me to the surface and on our way; I saw the same fish that I saw first. When I asked her about how they got here, she replied rudely "It's all because of you humans that destroyed our habitats and killed us for their own sake." Hearing these words really put a stone on my heart. Then I met some more animals and that reindeer-like-animal, Irish elk. It was really the most beautiful

animal that I had ever seen in my entire life. I saw an Asian straight-tusked elephant, Miyako row deer, wooly rhinoceros and many other animals that got extinct because of human faults.

I realized that human are so cruel and selfish that they destroyed these animals' habitats for the sake of their own luxury. *So, here I am standing in front of you warning you as well as educating you that every animal has their own life and home. So, care for them and protect them from being extinct. It's your duty. Save their life to be saved by God!!*

X

BIOG 10- SATYA PRAKASH SAHOO

Once a great man said," move in silence and only speak when it's time to say checkmate ." As in chess, Queen plays a vital role

with innumerous paths to go on , he has created a maze in his head. His belief on the fact that moving his footsteps in the direction of shuttle with a racket in his hand, proves to be an escape from the chaos. Dreaming feels like heaven, but with closed eyes and a nearly unconscious body. His generally showcase a guy in a white pinafore, with a surgical mask over his face, in an operation theatre. The sprinkles descending from the clouds, making the soil moist is the most comforting site to his tiny eyes. SRC, the most undetachable emotions, to him while gave his life the meaning his name 'SATYA PRAKASH' holds. He is a person with the best co-ordination and unity

THE SLOW POISONING OF THE ARCTIC- THE POLLUTION

My day starts with collecting polythene, plastic cans,wrappers,from the water bodies it may be ponds, lakes etc. One gloomy morning when I was sleeping. 'Thud' a sound came from outside. And i woke up hurriedly by getting scared about the sound. I thought to go and check what is going on outside, I was very scared because the sound was very loud. So, I sat in corner of my cave and didn't move from there. After some time I felt hungry and thought to go out. I was still thinking of that loud sound in my mind. After waiting for some minutes I arose courage to go out and check everything is fine or not. Like an ant I walked towards the face of the cave and i saw there was a huge ice ball in front of my cave. By seeing that I came to know that there was a melting of a big mountain and all this was caused for humans only. "This disgusting humans", I shrieked 'This homosapiens can never be changed', I shouted. They always have been tried to destroy this pleasing environment. What did they

get by polluting the environment? If after being a polar bear I can think then, why not this human can think about this?

While searching for food I'm thinking of destruction caused by humans. The environment was highly affected due to global warming cause by those blather homosapiens and the main cause are "Green house effect, nuclear power plant, radio active defilement , nuclear weapon testing because all these produces poisonous gases and heat. The unnecessary wars also produce more poisonous gases and large amount of heat. The war only doesn't affect the place where it had occurred, it also affect the whole world especially arctic region. Day to day the environment is polluted by, daily using things such as vehicles, refrigerator and many other electric devices because all this produces carbon monoxide, methane, nitrous oxide which are very poisonous to environment. Due to this their was a hole created in ozone layer, the layer which protect us from UV rays.

Having heard a noise from distant place, I rushed to know what's happening there. I saw some researchers were enjoying their day. Behind them there was a huge suitcase with all the researched equipments. After a while they opened their suitcase and took out some food material wrapped with the foil. They threw the foil at that place and went away. After that some little polar bears in search of food reached and there found a few leftover food, which was there inside the plastic, as they were going to enjoy, suddenly I rushed to them and stopped them from eating that plastic and i unwrapped the plastic to feed them. After that they left that place. Then I thought to move a far distance.

After a while I reached near a sea where I saw a ship loaded with garbage, we polar bear are suffering from many of the organic process which affect our development, procreation and aptitude to fight with malady. It was not for the first time that I saw the ship, already a few years ago in the same way pollution has been created by the ship.

Then i could feel my stomach grumble loudly and after walking some distance I saw a sea shore. There too the ocean was polluted. One month ago there was an oil spills in the ocean due to which the aquatic animals were affected by poisonous water. And some polar bears and penguins after consuming those affected aquatic animals, they died. And it shows how the humans have been disturbing the water as well. Melting of ice and increasing level of sea water is creating problems in the survival of arctic animals in the modern age. It has been seen many of the species in the polar region but nowadays pollution is standing a great question mark for the livelihood rates. And this condition shows that one day we will be suffering a lot by the scarcity of fresh water.

"Human being cannot survive without any other creatures. Instead other creatures can survive without homo-sapiens. Then why they are losing themselves and their generation? " By saying this I moved to other place in search of food. There I found a pond and went near it. I thought it was the end of my struggle for hunger. I caught a fish from pond. I tried for second time but in the second try I caught a plastic. Then I remembered about my young one who used to play, catch fishes and his one smile makes my day. But once, while searching for fish, he ate a piece of plastic instead of fish which choked him. Just because of that, he is no more in this world. And this is the only reason for which I was collecting plastic since ten years.

I thought that the accident occurred with my son should not occur with anyone else. And the second reason for collecting the plastic was I thought that a day will come when human will have some common sense and will stop polluting water. I'm still alive waiting for the day when I will return back to my cave without getting plastic in my surrounding. But these homosapiens will never change and will continue to pollute the water.

It was the day of storm, I was wandering here and there for a shelter and went more over for my bread. The hailstorms were falling on my furs. It felt like the cloud was stabbing it's icy nails on me. Gradually the temperature of my body started imbalancing due to my peckish belly. More and more over my eyes were closing like a lid of the hotpot. I could feel the last breath that passed through my nostrils.

The polar bear died but his soul remained immortal in the icy reason of the globe. Not the foolish community of the humans but a polar bear could sense the approaching danger to the remote areas of the earth "THE ARCTIC". The polar bear represents a perfect example of the wildlife. The humans have a

well built intellect and yet remain inconsiderate to the poisoning of the sphere.

Will the humans just continue for the tenable of the man made resources but not worry for the sustenance of nature? Will the homosapiens ever realise about the valuable existence of in-sapiens? The last question that appeared to be arrived on my mind was " Will our mènage exist in the near future ??

XI

BIOG 11- ABHIGNYA ARPIT PRADHAN

A person's own strength is his willpower. I like to grow with my dedication in the field of humanitarian work and activity. As a pupil my energy sinks with love elegantly, talk triumphantly and elude royally. Nature provides me to learn as well as earn how to achieve the target of social life. Trying to get the extraordinary outcomes from the ocean of wisdom. I share and care from my family, friends and relatives being the stepping stones. I feel to

recollect the tranquility from the legends and the commons. Loving to utilise my minutes to help the poor, the needy or the neglected ones.

Very systematically an unnoticed event has been created in my life. Whenever I feel my parents reality in the focus of my future, it gives me an immense pleasure. In a nut shell the motto of my life is to bloom a glimpse of smile in my priceless face, that will be the biggest achievement of my vision. Abhigyan, which refers to the knowledgeable one is scholar at SCGs with endless dedication and hard labor.

YOUR BRAIN THE SMARTPHONE AGE- SCIENCE: A BOON OR CURSE

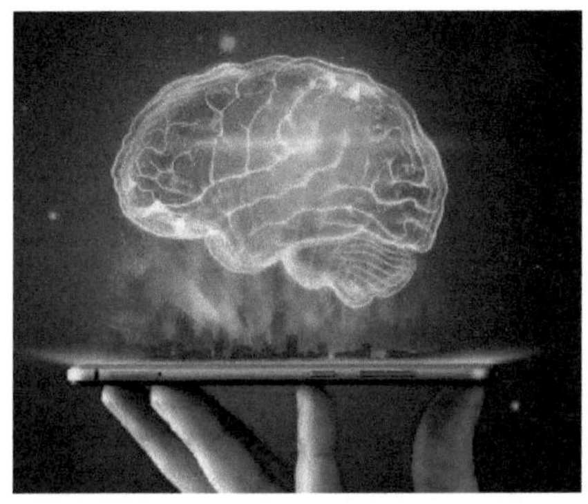

In the year of 2020 Sanjeev went to his grandfather's laboratory to call him for dinner and got some information about the experiment he was working on. At that evening his grandfather, Dr. Rohit Meher was trying to make a medicine for the incurable diseases like HIV, Cancer etc. But that day my grandfather was worried after reaching to his laboratory and he said to hide in the underground basement room.

After a few seconds there were sounds coming from grandpa laboratory about six to seven people were quarrelling against my grandpa and a few minutes later explosion caused in the grandpa laboratory and the chemical reaction caused in the

laboratory after explosion surged throughout the village and caused health problems in the people of village like sudden illness, paralysis, eyeburn , internal body pain and the village was almost filled with patients after seeing the crisis in the village after the explosion for the first time I thought that science can also cause destruction.

My family and I left the village after my grandfather's funeral, I promised myself to not engage in upcoming days in science and said "I want to learn about different cuisines of cooking" and my father replied "Do as you wish and I'll support your decision". I took the decision my self at the age of twelve.

After the twelve years in Japan, in Kanto, I was having a cooking battle against Yuga Takumi and the recipe is to prepare a dish with bear meat which has very bad odour after tasting. As it was a tough challenge to make a delicious dish of bear meat along with removal of odour. We both of us made a American fried recipe and we different techniques to make thc dish. I used flour with addition of rice crackers to make the meat crispy and inside the meat I used a winter fruit by mashing and adding the mashed fruit in it. As for Yuga he added spices to increase the fragrance and taste also countering the odour taste. After the judges decision I won with the support of two judges of three. Since for graduation I had three months for final test, I returned to India where I currently lived in a city after migrating the village in Mumbai.

Everyday I heard about cases of people dying in hospital in Mumbai due to unknown illness. This cases increased day by day after my friend in apartment got also affected and was fighting against life and death. After that case I became serious about interrogating about the cases as I saw report of the one who died with same diseases and his post mortem report and advanced post moterm report I saw strange chemical as I knew about those chemicals. I remember that my grandfather used to tell me about about the chemicals he used before the explosion and I wrote it on my notes and I remember that the notes in the storeroom wardrobe.

After reaching home I asked to mother, " Mom please lend me the key of storeroom for sometime". My mother replied, " Son, take it from the keystand that is on the wall". "Okay mom, I'll take it".

After I got the key of storeroom I opened the wardrobe and after a long search of two-three hours I got the notebook in my treasure box. After cross checking the report and the notebook I was shocked to see the chemicals that are inside dead body are same that were used for making the curation if disease which my grandpa worked on.

After that 7'o clock almost at night I went to meet the officer who was investigating about the cases and said him all about it. After a long discussion about the death of peoples cause he said mostly the people who good at stream like games, work or businesses by belittling people only got killed or hospitalized.

As I remember my friend, Sangram Tripathi who used bully with his weak football players. After remembering this I asked the officer Shinde, " Sir please allow me to work with you on the case". He replied, "Okay, you could be big help as you know the chemicals used on the hospitalized people and you have to co-operate with us".

"Yes sir I'll do anything to stop this crisis and find the culprit behind it". "Thank you for the help after giving the valuable information". " It's my pleasure sir, now sir we have to start advancing the and stop stop the culprit from doing".

Okay, 10AM tomorrow at morning, you reach at Leopold cafe and we will discuss about finding the culprit". " okay sir I will be present at 10AM". The next day I reached at Leopold cafe and one of his officer came in casual dress and said to follow him and I entered their hidden room in abandoned building and saw the killed people places on the Mumbai map. I saw a formation of different letters showing 'KILL' in apartment or places names of those cases.

After I practiced that the last case was 'L' starting name of a apartment, I then suggested to search people belittling people around them. After a long search with the agents and spyes around the places and names starting with 'L' , We found a person in Laver Parel. After finding the person, we reached his place and at his room we saw that he was also infected by chemicals and we were too late to find him and also the camera doesn't clearly show his face as he was wearing a skull printed mask. After hospitalizing him we started to continue the investigation and again the culprit will start again with the names of places starting with 'K'.

That day I felt regretted for not being able to reach in time. Then the next day we started to research and spread our sources with more faster and I also started to find the places with starting letter 'K'. After three days we found a gangster with the same case in the slums and to be honest I wasn't willing to help him but to find the real culprit, we had to help and I reached to the place with my bike more faster than the officer and after finding his place I saw him getting injected with a syringe and the murderer wanted to erase the evidence but he sprayed peper spray and escaped. I chased after him after washing my eyes with the water in the jar and followed him with all my might. I chased him like a cat and was able to get hold of him.....and the i unmasked him and saw his face.

But he was still able to escape. Soon the officers arrived....but they were late.I went near them and said," sir i was unable to catch him, but i have seen his face"."I need a sketch artist to draw his face".

After hearing this, the officers were relieved...They immediately asked the best sketch artist to come.
"We should keep this matter from reaching the public or else they would be panicked" I suggested.

"yes, and give out the news for preparing the vaccine for this unknown disease" said officer Sindhe. Officer sindhe commanded all the sources to keep an eye for who would be the next victim.

We caught the culprit behind the murder of the local gangster and interoguted him for 3 hours and came to know that he worked for a certain organization which consisted about 72 people and surprisingly they all were either doctors or trainers of different hospitals.

I got angry for what they did, but still felt sorry for the problems they went through.Their intentions weren't wrong but the way they used their knowledge was wrong.

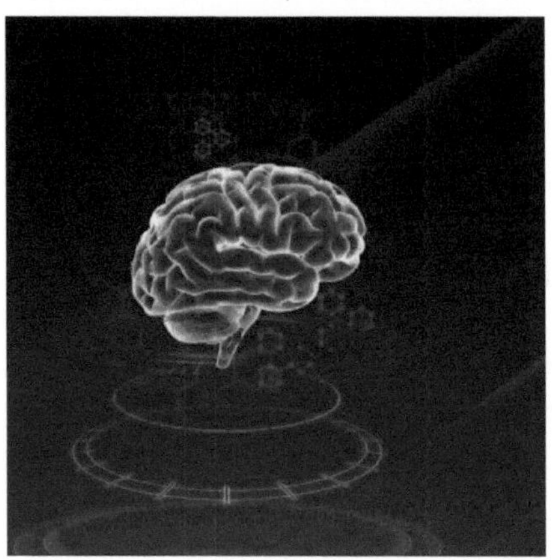

That organization tried to decrease the rate of crimes and bullies but they used science and those chemicals in a wrong way and failed my grandpa's good intentions.

XII

BIOG 12- ROHAN PATTANAIK

And unnoticed lad ,sitting ideally at a corner,who had no guts to even speak for a Jeffy; over time ,started being assigned to lead group and team at the school. This courage which emerged over the years seemed to be pheonix, born from its own ashes, the ash

beneath which a mystery is awaiting it's unleashment. The boy who lead an incessant life,who's mind it's overwhelming with thoughts who lives in a subconscious world while being in a conscious one. His silence makes people turn ignorant towards him but it also add up as a factor for his creativeness, it ignites his intellect and turn on the switch of curiosity in his brain. The reason behind joining SCGs was to acquire his dream on sitting infront of a well- equipped desk and level hanging at his door which would read,"Er. Rohan Pattanaik." But with a skull full of thoughts and disorganised verse, he considers writing as his passion.

"ODISHA"- THE LAND OF TEMPLES.

"UFF!!What a pic. I have to admit it that I actually click nice images." I exclaimed with joy standing on the peak of the Aravali .That moment was seemed like the moment in heaven .Then suddenly I fall from heaven on the ground when I realized that the last scheduled flight from Bundi. To Delhi is at 5:45 PM it was already 2:45 PM and the airport is 150 KM away from the location. Then I came down from the top of Aravali to the ground. And I found a cab to Bundi .But I luck was so in inauspicious that after 30KM the engine of the car got heated up smoke stared rise from the bonet . And unexpectedly the situation comes near me like a speed breaker than I have to take a lift from the highway to reach my destination. After reaching the airport, I rushed for my flight. I failed realized after sitting on my sit and stared scrolling my phone. Thereafter, I opened my vlog to click the comments on my previous video. I felled very happy to see my fan following

and the motivative comment which ignited me to upload more videos .On reaching home; I directly fall asleep on my bed.

Awaking on the next morning first I started thinking for the theme of my next vlog .Suddenly, a notification like a shooting star in the dark night came to my phone. While I enquired about the notification, there I found one of my fan suggest me to upload a vlog on temples. I thought about it and decided to go for it.

To make sure where I should go, I brought the globe and I rotated it. after which I closed my eyes and with the help of my fingers I selected a place as soon as I opened my eyes my finger was indicated on Odisha . Then I decided to go there for the new vlog.

Thinking about the place of Odisha I scheduled remembered my previous videos where I met a person and he also suggested me to visit Odisha preciously when I was there. But I ignored his after one week I took my flight from Delhi to Bhubaneswar. Reaching there I found the climate was different from Delhi from where I belong. In Bhubaneswar there is very less pollution as compared to New Delhi .Then I was trying to book a cab for my hotel room, suddenly my phone normal price forcibly I have to agree with the cab driver. And finally I reached my hotel room. Then after taking rest I started seeing my vlog chart, and then I asked my fan from Odisha to inform me about some significant temples of Odisha. Within 5 mins they all give me the information about the temples. From which I decided to go selected temples.

From the list I first decided to visit "SHREE MANDIR" which is one of the"CHAR DHAM". Thereafter I started my journey to Puri. After getting into the cab I stared my vlog.

".....Hello......guys it's your Yash is going to present a new vlog. I reached Odisha yesterday on your demand of a vlog on temples. I

am going to visit some temples of Odisha and its spiritual believes. Now as you can see that I have arrived at Puri .I am on my way in search of ashram where I can know about the "SHREE MANDIR", history and its believes .

"On the foot path I am walking in search of Ashram. Now a Baba is coming towards me. I asked "Baba where can I take rest for a while."He further asked "Where are you from?"I replied "I am from Delhi" and he told "Please come along with me."He showed me a place where I can take rest .I rested there for half hour."

I enquired about the SHREE MANDIR from that Baba he told that the " Lord Jaganath or "The Kaila" as emanated from the left burnet outwards of the "Chita" of load Krishna which was found by king Ananthavarma Chodaganga from Ganga River . The day when he found the wood, Lord Jaganath came to his dream and told him to make ideal of lord Jagganath . "Indradyumna" a famous culturist was assigned for making the sculpture of the lord Jaganath . "Baba also told me not to get surprised after seeing that the sculptures do not have full hands. Because when the sculptures were making the sculpture he told not to open the door of the room until he comes out himself. The sculptures were working on the ideal so the sound was coming out of the room. But after few days suddenly sound stopped. He also was not eating food which was given to him. So the guards in form, it to the queen. She walked into the room with the food as she thought that he might be ill. When she opens the door she saw the sculptures of Lord Jagannath, Maa Subhadra and lord Baladev without full hands.

Baba told that "The temple is 65 meter (213-feet) tall. It has 31 small temples inside the temple premises".

“Then Baba suggested, you must unite the temple. And worship Kalia?”

“Now I’m on the way to the Shree Mandir. I’m entering the temple and climbing the twenty two stairs called “Baisi Bacha”.with each step I’m feeling the positive vibes are coming towards me like tidal waves. Now I am entering the “Rekhadula”.

Now you can see the almighty, the lord of the world, “Mahaprabhu Jagannath”. Now I’m coming out of the Deula. I’m sitting under the shadow of the Shree Mandir. Oh the moment I looked into the eyes of the “”Mahaparabhu, It felt like my soul is getting purified. All my inferior Karma’s are getting inverted into good Kormas”. “Seeing the at the top of the temple waving in the opposite direction of wind “I got shocked and I ask myself how it is possible.” The shadow of the temple is on one direction only through the day.

“Oh Man, my tummy is growling like dog. I’m very much hungry at the moment. I must have some food before I get senseless. Yes, I remember that Baba was talking about” “Maha Prasad” has is income parable with any of the foods served in 5 star I also tasting “Pheni of which I’ve heard from all over the Puri”

On the way back to the Ashrom,”I am thinking about the Arunn Stamba” and inside the temple there is “Goruda Stamba”. As I per my knowledge the “ Vahrna” is the “Vahanna” of Lord Surya. So, I am going to ask about it to the Baba.

I asked “Baba why the Aruna stamba is situated outside the temple not inside and why it is situated outside surya temple as it is the vahaana of Lord surya”

My curious mind is forcing me to visit the Konark temple.

"Hey friend, now I'm not Konark- which is known as the Sun temple. The first scene, I'm see the front look and it is looking like a chariot. Here is tour guide let have a conversation with him."

I asked, "Guide Dada do you know anything about the Aruna Stamba?" Guide Dada replied" "Yes Arun Stamba was on part of the Konark Temple."

I asked "Then why was it shifted to Shree Mandir."

Guide Dada replied "It was inside the Deula where the ideal of Lord Surya was hanging in air because of the magnets which were later dismantled by the Britisher due to which the temple started to break into pieces. So they have to shift the stamba from Konark to Shree Mandir".

Now I'm standing in the lawn beside the temple and trying image the size of the temple which was destroyed by bruisers.

Next stop Bhubaneswar. "Now I've returned to Bhubaneswar- The temple city of Odisha. First, I am going to book a room and rest over there for 5-6 hrs."

I'm at Lingraj temple which is one of the biggest temple in Bhubaneswar. In temple Lingraj both Lord Shiva and Lord Vishnu are worshipped. Here "Maa Paravati" is known as "Bhubaneswari" and "Lord Shiva" is known as "Lingaraj". The temple seems a little shorter than Shree Mandir. The main tower is 51 meter tall. This temple is dedicated to Goddess Bhagawati in the North-western corner of the temple. There are more than 180 small temples inside the temple premises. There is a beautiful garden Ekamra Keshetra. It took 3-4 hours to visit the whole temple".

"The time it's the turn for "Maa Cuttack Chandi" which is situated at Cuttack-The silver city".

"Let talk with a citizen of Cuttack".

Which Puja's are famous in "Maa Cuttack Chandi?" I asked

Citizen replied "Maa Cuttack Chandi dedicated to goddess Chandi. Maa Cuttack Chandi, rules on the hearts of the ancient city. Maa Cuttack Chandi is famous for Durga Puja & Kali Puja".

I am inside the temple of Maa Cuttack Chandi, the smell of the "Jhuna" inside the temple is just purifying anything entering inside the temple. There I worshipped Maa Cuttack Chandi and returning to the room.

"Hi guys, Last but not the least I've arrived at "Ghata Gaon Tarani", If the outer look of it was so beautiful, then imagine how beautiful it will be from inside. Now I am entering the temple. The surrounding inside, is like I am in heaven. There are 3 temples inside the Tarini temple. After visiting the main temple, I visited the rest two. I now taste the Tarini Pitha".

"Ok, guys that's enough for this vlog. I think you will like the vlog and please share your views in my comment section. See you soon in my next vlog".

XIII

BIOG13- HRISHITA DAS

The honk's of the ships never let sleep till late, as a child. After consummating puberty, her incumbency, obligation, commitment didn't. Being the elder daughter in a Bourgeois is no so easy, she potrays this fact really well. Her dedication is as high as the everest she laughs the laughter of an angle. House craft comports her along with the reactions of organic Chemistry. Nacl

rich breeze could not wear away her glamour ever. Diwali, Eid, Christmas, Guru Nanak Jayanti, she finds peace and frenzy for every fiesta. Starring at the scriptures and applaucling at them for hours never seems like a time waste. Hrishita's dad is everything to her. SCGs has gave her a vision, motivating her to work harder with each passing day. A dream of being called us Dr. Das has remain intact since ages in her heart.

HINDU TEMPLE AS A SOCIAL INSTITUTION

The repeated schedule of every morning had got into my nerves. The exactly same routine, with each passing day. My frustration was at its peak. I was bored, severally bored of everything. I wanted, no, I needed a change. A change for my own good. Hence I decided to visit my Grandpa who lived alone in the village. And suddenly the last bell of the day rang and the school got over.

I came back and was completely alone at home. My parents were out mostly, for their work. I was bored of the food prepared everyday at home. So, I ordered some online. As, the order was placed, playing video game seemed to be a good option, until the food was delivered. The door bell rang and I ran to open the door it was the delivery boy.

After that I watched a series of drama while eating the Pizza, Burger with some coke. After some time again the bell rang and I saw in my phone it was around 5 PM. it's the time for my mother's return. After opening the door I went into my room to get ready for tution. While getting ready for tution I heard some sound from the dinning room. Oh ! It's my Mummy shouting at me because I didn't clean the dinning after eating but ignoring her words, I took the bag and went out of the house.

Around 7.30 PM. I returned home and directly went to my room and started playing video games. Around 9.15 PM again I heard the bell ringing and that was my Papa at the door. After some time my mother called me for dinner. And that time I was thinking from which day summer vacations will start. Within fractions of second a message flashed on my phone's screen, from school I that due to order from Government the summer vacation starts from tomorrow. After reading that message I felt like "Yes, it's the time to relax". Then I went to the dining room for dinner and dad was already present there we all sat for dinner. I informed them about the summer vacation.

"Mummy, Papa there was message from school that the summer vacation are starting from tomorrow". I informed.

"Have you been assigned any home work ?" Papa asked.

"No Papa", I said.

"Mummy, Papa, I want to pay a visit to grandpa at village I expressed"

"What are you going to do in village" Papa asked.

"Stay here your school has summer vacation but tutions are still gonna continue ! Mummy said"

"Tution are also off for 20 day's I said angrily"

And at that moment there was a call on my Papa's phone. It was grandpa, He expressed his wish to see me and asked Papa to sent me to his house at village and both my parents agreed to leave me at the village.

I ran to my room to pack my luggage for village. The very next morning I caught the bus and went to my village, as soon as I reached my grandpa's house I saw him waiting for me with his walking stick in his hand and standing outside the house. I went near him and greeted him by saying Good afternoon, Grandpa, later on we both went inside the house.

Grandpa cooked my favorite dishes and we both enjoyed while taking our lunch then grandpa did everything but I directly went to bed and started watching movies. Grandpa asked me to take rest but I didn't gave importance to his words. At evening grandpa prepared snacks and offered me to eat. After evening snacks grandpa told me to study but a I told him I don't want to study and I started using phone.

We finished our dinner and then grandpa went to bed but I was still watching. phone and at around 2.30 AM grandpa wake up but he saw me still using phone and he asked me to sleep and I went bed.

At 5.00 AM in the morning grandpa woke up and saw that I was sleeping this type of attitude of mine continued for 3 to 4 days. On the 5 days grandpa asked me to get ready and accompany him to visit a place, I followed him until we reached a temple, them I doubtfully asked, "Grandpa why are we here ?"

Me and my grandfather set out for the temple. As we interred the holy place, I save many children rowed up on the floor. In front of them sat a man in a dhoti and that's the moral of the story, "He said, It get we curious but regardless, I followed my grandfather".

"Just wait for me here." My grandfather said as he walked away towards of priest. I looked at the beautifully carved ceiling.

"Bhoomi ! Come here". My grandfather called out I walked over to him.

"Look at them." He indicated towards the children that I had seen previously.

"That is a 'shivir' being held by the temple".

Various things are taught here. And I want you to join it.

"But"-

"No but Bhoomi" he interrupted me.

We walked over to the gathering.

"Come sit here", said the priest standing behind us. Me and my grandfather sat on the floor besides the other kids. I sat there for around fifteen minutes. "When are we going to leave, grandpa?" I whispered out with grim face. "Already bored? Wait for a few more minutes!", said grandpa.

"Hey. You! You kid over there! Come here. Listen to me for a moment!" said the priest. I looked at grandpa nervously.

"Go. Give it a try."

I walked over to the priest.

"Here are five kids. You lead them. You will be given a mission with a deadline. You are supposed to complete the mission within the given period of time."

I was not at all expecting this. First of all a temple and now some stupid mission!

"Pick up a chit from the pot kept over there. And find the mentioned stuff along with your team." He said

“What is written in that chit?” priest asked

“There is a question” I replied

“Ok Bhoomi lead your team for the mission” priest commanded

Lead ur team .... But I have never been a leader before ! Can l do it ? How should I interact with them ? These thoughts struck me after listening to the priest words

And then a girl from my team called me I looked at her.

'Hey I am Ayisha' she introduced herself politely

'Hey I am Bhoomi' I replied

After that we started talking.And then we met other 3 teammates

' Hey I am Suresh, he is Mohit , she is Shradha ' they introduced themselves

'Hey I am Bhoomi' I introduced myself

Then we started talking. I thought I had a fear of interacting with others but now I was talking with them like we all were friends since 5 year and then I Ayisha came near to me and Jerked me and asked 'where are you and what are you thinking?'

'Nothing' I replied. After that priest came and all teammates stood up I didn't know why they stood up then 'Boomi stand up 'I heard it was Ayisha's voice ' Bhoomi stand up ' she commanded "it is to respect Elders"

Then I also stood up

Priest said " complete your mission with in 15 minutes.

Listening this much, all started giving the point of view for the question. Suddenly my eyes fall on Ayisha she was standing quietly and thinking . So, I went near to her to ask what she was thinking off. She said " let's work in unity" . After her Suresh also said " yes ,let's work in unity" From there I came to know How to work in Unity. From our team Mohit was of ST caste and Suresh was of General but they doesn't discriminate among themselves and we all work very hard didn't got the answer of priest question and in melancholy mood we are returned back to Temple but when do you reached Temple we saw priest was waiting for us with big smile . We all felt sorry but he gave a gift to each of us but we all doesn't understand what was going on? And then the priest asked" what did you learned from this?" we all doesn't understood what he was asking for?

"UNITY" Suresh said

" Cooperation with everyone" Ayisha said

"No no discrimination between caste and colour" I said

" Communication skills" Shradha said

" Trust " Mohit said

" Yes, my dear this is the main knowledge you learnt ft this mission. you didn't failyou all won to mission" priest answered with a wide smile . After listening this much fun priest we all gave a wide smile to each other .We got back to the grandpa house. There I narrated every incident to him . He felt happy by seeing me happy and I told my grandpa that I will go temple everyday for the social knowledge and everyday I 'll gain one social knowledge .Then day by day I left my phone to totally and was addicted with study and with my own work and help my grandma in free time I give my most of time to my grandpa and like this the end of the summer vacation came . I had a good bonding with everyone in the temple and we five became best friends and we used to share very very little things also.

I had very much fun and had learnt many things from the temple .Like this my last day came in the village .I was feeling very bad and was about to cry for living them and going back to Own home then my grandpa was also sad because I'm going back to my City then I came back to my home and same alone at home but this time I did every work of the house decorated my room I cleaned every room as my mother didn't get time to clean all the room and then I went to kitchen room and I saw nothing was cooked that day because that day it was half day of my mother .But I decided to cook that day and I cooked and then ate something After some time my mother came to home and she was shocked after seeing all this .She directly came to my room and saw I was studying 'Bhoomi' she called me

I turn around her and when near to hear and touched her feet and said Namaste.

She lift up me and hugged me and then I went with her and served her food which I had cooked and we had a leisure time together and I narrated my experience in village this time . She became very happy after seeing me changed

Temple are said spiritual institution .No they are not only spiritual institution but also a social institution we all go many institution for studies and there we spend lakh lakh money but didn't get any social manner but in temple we came to know about social manners such as charity, helping others, giving respect to elders etc. In my life Temple actually work as social institution not only in my life it also work as social institution in many's life

XIV

BIOG 14- RAHUL DEV BERA

With versatility flowing through his veins, seated on the RBCs , he is a guy brought up in the lap of mother nature . He is a childish teenage with the no granted freedom ,now approaching towards adulthood . With his flattering smile and so clearly polite access, this Rahul can win over not only "Tina", but any girl around him.

He's the most well behaved and scholastic individual of his batch. Sight of a flock of sparrows flying over his head, a stream of water flowing through the rocks after descending from a waterfall delights eye-appealing young man the most. During the India vs Pakistan tournament, he is one to reserve the front seat. His gesture never fails to impress his colleagues and tutors at SCGS. One of the most down to Earth soul you would ever see.

PREHISTORIC- THE SHRINE

Tin... tin... tin...

The alarm clock sounds, "Oh Man ! It's already late".

I got ready hurriedly within five minutes. I ran to school, with my sandwich in my mouth. "UFF... thank god. I arrived at the school in time". The day passes out like a minute, but at the end of the day as it was the final working day of year, our vacations is going to form tomorrow & as an holiday project, we are given a topic on Ancient Architectural Shrines. Being average student the project seem like a punishment, as all my planning were going to be white washed and in was mandatory to prepare the project for the sake of twenty marks, which will be further added on the Annual Examinations. Now it's the time for the closing of

school.

I returned to home like a warrior, who is returning from war, after getting victory. When I reach to the home my father, who watching TV asked me to sit beside him, the though which was bouncing inside my brain was that my father is going to scold, but all my thoughts proved wrong in spite of scolding me my father started to try to make me understand the value of time, He told me a like that "If your respect time than, time will respect you, If you will not respect time than time will surly rain you someday". Those words from my father ignited the fire insight me. After getting into my room, I freshen up & thinking about my project till I fall asleep.

Next morning, I wake up & got freshen, asked mother for the help in "Holiday Project". After listening my mother suggested to meet my uncle, who is a renowned archeologist. She asked. "Why don't you contact with your uncle?" He will surely help you in this project & you will also about complete you project with enjoyment".

I called up my uncle immediately and enquired whether he was free for the project". the replied yes, son I am always ready for you.

After a day I took train. From Mumbai to Delhi, my uncle reached up to station for picking me & we together drive to Anandvihar where my uncle living. My Aunt asked,

"How are you, Bisal"

I replied "I am fine".

"Come let's go for dinner" Aunt said.

After taking dinner I directly went to my bed.

On the next morning, Uncle woke me up & he told me,

"Let's go for morning walk", asked me "How is your study going on?"

I replied, "It's going as usual, but I have got a project which s giving me headache. Because I didn't have any idea about it."

My uncle further asked about the topic of the project,

I replied it is all about "Ancient Architectural shrines".

Uncle said, "Oh, don't worry I will surly help you in the project"

After the meaning walk, We came to home & freshen up.

At that time Aunt called us for the breakfast, the breakfast was so delicious that it made my mood changed & I became cheerful.

Ten minutes later.

My uncle told, "Come on Bishal, lets discus on project".

I entered to my uncle's room; uncle asked me "What do you mean by shrine, do you have any idea about it".

I nodded my head.

My uncle told, "Don't worry; just listen to my words".

"Shrine is a holy place, where the people if different mindset & religions pray there God, for the save of life."

"Let me tell you some ancient Shrines of India, According to Indian mythology the "Rameswaram", which is a part of "Dhams", When Adi Shankaracharya was popularizing the idea of Hindu Philosophy, he established these four dhams / mathas i.e. Shardha pith in Srinagar, Kalika Pith in Dwarika, Jyoti Pith in Badrinath & Govrdhan pith in Jagannath Puri".

"I questioned, how the temple was made?”

"According to the Ramayana, Lord Rama had established, Rameswarm to absolve the sins greeted in Sri Lanka, Lord Rama wanted to have a large Lingum of Shiva to worship, So, he directed to Lord Hanuman for the purpose, but as Hanuman was late in bringing the Lingum, Devi Sita made as mass Shiva Lingum of sand available at Seashore. The Lingum made by Devi sita was named s Ramalingum & the state brought by Lord Hanuman afterword was named as "Viswalingum. Both the lingas were established by lord Rama". Responded Uncle.

I eagerly questioned, "Uncle can you describe about the structural architecture".

He said, "The Rameswaram Temple is spread over an area of 15 areas & has been built in the style called "Dravidian" the beams, Pillars and ceilings are made made-up of the sandstone with great architectural designs. This temple as mainly made up of Granite from huge Granite rocks. These mainly have 2 large Pyramidal towers the east one is 78ft. height with 5 tiers and the other one was in west in 126ft high of 9 tires."

Then I asked, "My uncle for the next temple".

Uncle rejoined "You can find many Shrines all over the India but Kedarnath is one of then . The saint of the Kedarnath often tell about the gleaning of names of Kedarnth, that in order to save from demon Lord Shiva manifest itself as a disguised bull & began to destroy demons with horns & hooves at that time, he said "Kodarum". It means whom to tear about from that word "Kodarum" the name Kedarnath derived.

"Uncle and you please say about its architecture."

"It is a temple made up of stones of gray huge. The temple was made with interlocking the stones with each other. There are no motor used in this, this temple is at a height of 358m from the rishikesh". The temple is a magnificent architectural design in all over the India".

My uncle pursued about one more architect motif that is Haji Ali Dargarh.

He proceed that, "According to the Islamism Haji Ali Dargarh was constructed in the memories of Sayyed gave up all his patrimony for the construction of mecca. It was set up in 15th century at 1431. It is built on a tiny archipelago located 500m from the coast. This archipelago is linked to a city prescient of Mahalaxmi by a narrow quay, which was nearly 0.62 miles long. This temple occupier the marble countryard containing central Shrine". The tomb within the Moscow is covered with sheet of red & green the main hall was of the full of mirror designs in haleidosoopic patterns in a Arabic patterns. During any high tides of the ocean the Dargarh seems to be no access.

After this I became free from all stress because I have finally accomplished the holiday project. So now I can enjoy my holidays in my uncle's family.

SRI CHAITANYA- THE FLAME OF EDUCATION

Sri Saichaitanya Global School, is the brain child of National Integrated Caring Education Trust.

MESSAGE FROM THE DIRECTOR

we have achieved a lots of milestones and helped thousands of successful student in launching their career. All the time, we are putting our best efforts to bring the best to the students. Sri Chaitanya has built hundreds of success stories and helped students to achieve their goals since its inception.

OUR MISSION

Our mission is to prepare students to be fully equipped with all knowledge in our fast-paced changing society. We will also lead in educating students about diversity that will enable them to better understand our differences, to unite and respect each other. We will ensure that our students develop their skills and intellectual competencies that are essential for success and leadership in the future. To bring change in quality education of weaker, deprived and vulnerable students and to make them scholars through participatory education and for their welfare development programs.

OUR VISION

Our vision is to develop confident, responsible and well mannered students who aspire to achieve their full potential. We will do this by providing a diverse, secured, fun and supportive learning environment in which everyone is equal and all achievements are celebrated.

A Page Of Response And Views, If Any

Printed by Libri Plureos GmbH in Hamburg, Germany